Nestlé smarties

ALL THE

INCREDIBLE FACTS

YOU EVER NEED TO KNOW

ALL THE
INCREDIBLE
FACTS
YOU EVER NEED TO KNOW

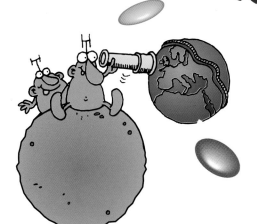

text by Mike Ashley

illustrations by David Mostyn

Robinson Children's Books

Thank you, friends

This book took a lot of work to get together. I couldn't have done it without the help of a lot of good friends and without a continual supply of Smarties. Special thanks go to writer and editor Paul Barnett and writer and nuclear physicist David Langford, both of whom read and commented upon the manuscript for this book. I must also thank Mary Reed, who provided much specialist help on weather matters and helped me find amazing things on the internet. Thanks also go to Liz Cruwys, for her special knowledge of the Antarctic; Donna Stevens of the Planetary Society; Donald K. Yeomans of the Jet Propulsion Laboratory for facts on comets; Dr Norbert Untersteiner and Dr Richard Armstrong for amazing snow facts; Mark Atterton of the World Conservation Monitoring Centre for facts on endangered animals; and Carl Haub for help on the total number of people who have ever lived; not forgetting of course Nestlé for making all the Smarties. Finally thanks to Nova Jayne Heath of Robinson Publishing for getting this show on the road, and to David Mostyn for bringing the facts alive.

Some facts remain true from generation to generation. For example, we know that the Earth spins around the Sun. But other facts change day by day – like the number of people living in India. Sometimes, even facts believed to be true for hundreds of years can be proved wrong, in fact before the 1500s most people believed that the Sun spins around the Earth. Our view of things can change as knowledge emerges and there will always be new incredible facts to amaze us. All the facts in this book were as accurate as possible when it went to press.

Abbreviations used in this book.

mm = millimetre	km/h = kilometres per hour
cm = centimetre	g = gram
m = metre	kg = kilogram
km = kilometre	°C = degrees Celsius

For reference to large numbers see page 69.

First published in the UK by Robinson Children's Books,
an imprint of Robinson Publishing Ltd, 1999

Robinson Publishing Ltd
7 Kensington Church Court
London W8 4SP

Text © Mike Ashley 1999
Illustrations © David Mostyn 1999
Typeset and coloured by Oxford Designers & Illustrators
NESTLÉ and SMARTIES are registered trademarks
of Société des Produits Nestlé S.A., 1800 Vevey, Switzerland.
© 1999 Société des Produits Nestlé S.A., Vevey, Switzerland. Trade Mark Owners.

A copy of the British Library Cataloguing in Publication Data for this title is available from the British Library.

ISBN 1 84119 068 3

10 9 8 7 6 5 4 3 2 1

Contents

Introduction 6 – 7

Body Bits — Lots of yucky and totally amazing facts about you and your body. 8 – 19

Amazing Animals and Stupendous Plants — Really incredible facts about plants and animals which are even more staggering than humans! 20 – 31

Monsters from the Past — All about gigantic and not so gigantic dinosaurs and other incredible creatures from the ancient past. 32 – 41

What's Out There? — The most amazing facts about outer space – the stars, planets and the Universe. 42 – 51

What on Earth!? — Staggering facts about the Planet Earth; awesome oceans, exploding mountains, shuddering earthquakes and much more. 52 – 63

Spectacular Science — Here are the really smart facts about super-science and mad scientists! 64 – 71

Mysterious X-Files — Super-spooky facts about ghosts, monsters and other unknown weird stuff! 72 – 79

What Did They Really Do for Us? — Unbelievable facts about some of the maddest, cleverest, oldest, youngest, smelliest and most dangerous people who have lived over the last 10,000 years! 80 – 89

There and Back Again — Lots of pretty cool facts about travel and exploration – the fastest, furthest and oddest transport! 90 – 101

The Human Touch - People and Places — Humungous facts and figures about the billions of people on the Earth, and the weird places they live. 102 – 109

Fun and Games — This is where the fun really starts, with hundreds of incredible facts and figures about sports, games and entertainment. 110 – 119

Oddities and Entities — And finally a pile of really amazing facts that belong nowhere but that you just have to know – the most amazing things you could ever believe! 120 – 127

Index 128

HEY! CAN YOU BELIEVE THIS?

OK Smartiepants – so I suppose you think you know it all already!

Well, we all know that Smarties are incredible: there are lots and lots of them, they're colourful, great to play with and very very scrummy. BUT did you know . . .

- Nearly 17,000 Smarties are eaten every minute in Britain alone.
- It takes 22 hours to make just one Smartie, but only a few seconds to eat one.
- It would take over 1,270 billion Smarties to fill Wembley Stadium.
- And all those Smarties would weigh over 1.25 million tonnes!
- What's more, all of those Smarties would wrap around the Earth over 470 times!

OK, so that's all pretty astonishing – but now it's time to prepare yourself! You are about to be really astounded and amazed . . .

GET THIS!

If everyone in Britain ate Smarties at the same time they could eat 1,270 billion Smarties in just eighty seconds!

Did you know . . .

- That there's enough water inside you to wash a car?
- A day on Venus is longer than its year.
- That Concorde flies nearly as fast as the Moon orbits the Earth!

That's just 3 out of thousands of amazing facts you'll find in this book.

Years ago I was astonished when I discovered that the world's biggest tree weighs around 2,200 tonnes, which is 14 times heavier than the world's biggest animal. And I was even more astonished to realize that the nearest star was so far away that it would take almost 18,000 years to get there!

It's these kinds of incredible facts that make me want to know more about the Universe and our amazing world, and that's what this book is all about. You'll learn hundreds of really disgusting facts about your body, and totally amazing stuff about plants and animals, especially dinosaurs. There are staggering facts about the planet Earth and about other planets and stars. And there are really weird facts about science and mysteries and oddities. And there's lots, lots more . . .

If those facts amaze you then you'll be zonked out by what you'll find in this book. Pretty soon you'll be impressing your friends with all the incredible facts you ever want to know! I hope they are as incredible to you as they are to me.

Now, if you're a real Smartiepants see if you can turn any of these facts into Smartie facts:

If an elephant can weigh up to 8 tonnes (8000kg), and a Smartie weighs approximately 1g (0.001kg), how many Smarties would you need for the weighing scales to balance?

Or
If the tallest tree is 100m high, and the length of one Smartie tube is 13cm long (0.13m), how many tubes would you have to stand on top of each other to reach the top of the tree?

See how many other facts you can turn into Smartie facts (answers to the ones above are at the end of the book).

Have fun!

Mike Ashley

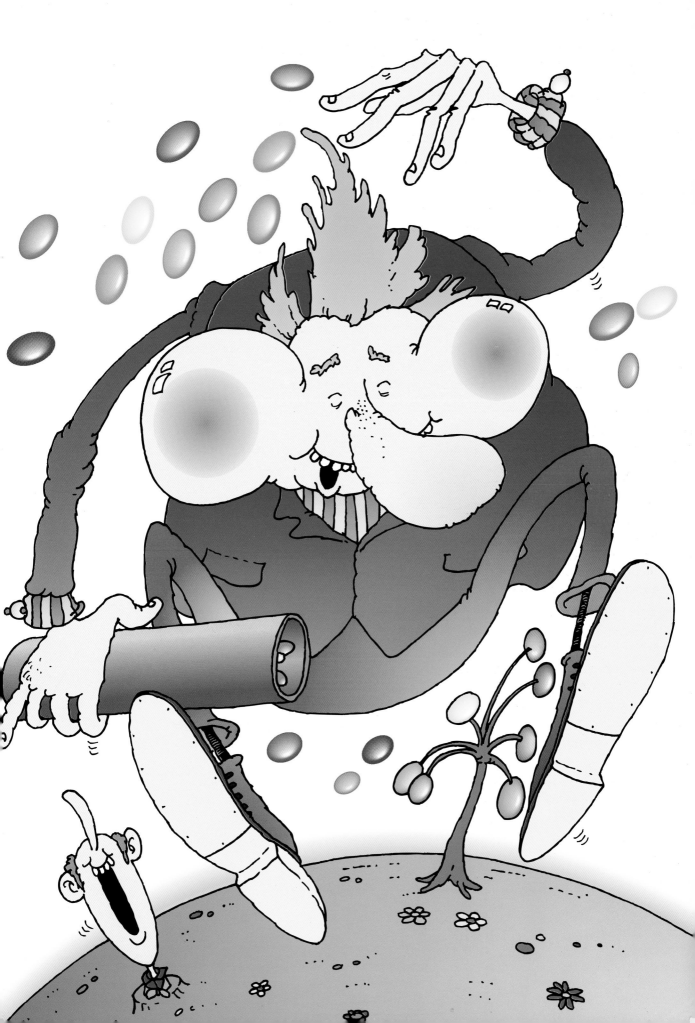

BODY BITS

Your body is amazing. It's got lots of bits, some of them incredible and others incredibly yucky. Sometimes you might be ill – and then it's even yuckier. Yet most of the time it looks after itself without you having to think about it.

But do you really know just how amazing your body is and what it's capable of? All those guts and mucky bits.

Did you know you produce nearly 1 litre of spit every day?

And when you sneeze bits whizz out of your nose as fast as an Intercity express train.

Did you know you're covered in lots of tiny little bugs and creepy-crawlies – and without them you'd be smelly and really grotty, because they clean you up.

There's lots like that going on all over you, and inside you, every minute of the day.

Let's crawl all over the body and see what we can find.

Pin-head

Your body is made up of 75 trillion (75,000,000,000,000) cells. They're all different shapes and sizes but it would still take 10,000 cells to cover the head of a pin. So you're equal to 7.5 billion pin-heads.

BUT, we haven't finished yet. Each cell is made up of 90 trillion (90,000,000,000,000) atoms. So your body has 675,000 times more atoms than there are stars in the entire Universe.

New cells for old

Every minute, 3 billion of your cells die, yet your body's so clever it replaces almost all of them straight away.

Almost all the cells in your body are completely replaced about every 7 years. So you may no longer have any of the same cells you were born with.

Oil and water

There's enough water and fat inside you for a long, soapy bath, or to wash a car.

Your body is 70% water. It contains 38 litres – that's about half a bathful. And . . .

there's enough fat in your body to make seven bars of soap.

Brain box

This is where all the work goes on. Your brain is better than the most brilliant computer. Yet it weighs only about as much as a cabbage (1.4kg) and looks like a monster walnut pickled in rhubarb juice. The top part of the brain – the gungy bit that looks like bendy pipes – is the bit that keeps you thinking and moving. If you unravelled it all it would just about cover your bed. You could use it as a bedspread, but it might pong a bit after a day or two.

In charge

One side of your brain is dominant over the other. You can tell which by whether you are left-handed or right-handed. Which are you? If you're left-handed then the right side of your brain is in charge, and you're more likely to be creative and artistic. If you're right-handed, the left side's in charge, and you're likely to be more logical and scientific.

The brain has 15 billion cells – that's about $2\frac{1}{2}$ times more cells than there are people in the world. And they're all at work all of the time – even when you're asleep.

Super-strong

How much do you weigh? If you're fit and strong, 40% of your weight is muscle. Muscle is heavier than fat, which is why really strong men weigh so much.

You have about 650 muscles in your body, and you use about 200 of them when you walk.

Shock patrol

Are you nervous? Do you jump when someone goes BOO? No, of course not! But your whole nervous system is looking out for you all the time.

There are 100 billion nerve cells (called neurons) inside you, all flashing on and off like traffic lights as messages are sent around the body.

These neurons are all spread out along 50,000km of nerves. That's enough to stretch $1\frac{1}{4}$ times round the Earth.

If you pulled the nerves out of everyone on Earth and strung them together, they'd stretch out into space almost as far as the star Arcturus – that's over 300 trillion km.

Warning signals and messages from the brain whizz along these nerves up to 576km/h. That's 16 times faster than Linford Christie in a 100m sprint.

Big mouth

The strongest muscles are the masseters, either side of the jaw. They help you bite and chew. They can exert a force of 80kg. But that's nothing compared with an alligator's jaws. They clamp shut with a force of almost 1,360kg!

Your biggest muscle is your gluteus maximus. It sounds more like a Roman general but it's the muscle in each of your buttocks. They're the muscles you bounce up and down on.

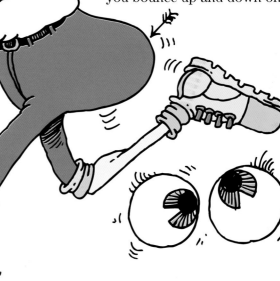

But the busiest muscles are the six that move each eye about 100,000 times every day. That's as much exercise as the leg muscles get on an 80km walk.

To find out what amazing things these muscles can do, turn to page 112, which looks at some super-human records.

Skinny bits

Your skin weighs about 2.5kg – but on a really fat person it can weigh as much as 5kg. If you peeled it off (yuck) and laid it out, it would cover a table-tennis table.

Most of what you see when you look at someone is dead. The outer layer of skin, their hair, their nails – it's all dead.

You shed about 40,000 dead skin cells every minute. That's enough to fill a small suitcase in a lifetime. Most of the dust in the air you breathe in is dead skin. Every time you blow your nose there's a little bit of your friends and family (and you) in your hanky! Bet you can't tell who's who!

That dead skin is tasty grub for dust mites. There will be over a million of them all round you now – in your chair, your bed, on the carpet - all chomping away on your dead skin.

Plus there are about 2 million bacteria on your face alone! And that's after you've washed.

Bony bits

Do you know you've got more bones than your parents? You're born with 305 and by the time you're their age 100 of those have joined up, and you're left with 206.

Most of those bones are in your hands and feet.

Greasy bits

Your sense of touch works through your skin. There are over 55 million sensory cells all over your body.

Every square centimetre of your skin has:

- 2.9 million cells
- 3,000 sensory cells
- 97 sweat glands
- 14 oil glands
- nearly 1m of blood vessels

. . . and lots of little bugs crawling all over it, eating the dead skin.

You may sweat about 1.7 litres of water every hour you're awake and about 0.3 litres when you're asleep. That's 10,000 litres every year – enough to fill 126 baths.

Gob smacked

You need spit to help digest food. You produce about 1 litre of saliva every day. That's 27,000 litres in a lifetime – enough to fill two swimming pools.

Your tongue is covered in taste buds, and you know what – you're tastier when you're young. As you get older you lose some of your taste buds. A baby has 10,000 taste buds but an adult has about 8,000.

Your taste buds are sensitive enough to identify 1 drop of lemon juice diluted in 129,000 drops of water.

Smelly facts

Your nose is full of mucus. It's the sticky liquid that traps all the muck and dust you breathe in and stops it getting into your lungs. In the end it has to come out. That's when you sneeze and all those horrible nose bits come flying out like an express train at 165km/h.

But there's still lots of mucus left. In fact you swallow about a quarter of the mucus your nose produces. (Ugh!) The rest wallows about, making you sniff.

I MOLECULE OF SKUNK PONG.

Nosey parker

At the very top of your nose, where the mucus collects, are over 50 million cells which are highly sensitive to smell. They're called olfactory receptor cells and each one can identify 1 odour molecule of the faintest or smelliest smell.

Your nose can distinguish between 4,000 and 10,000 different smells. It's so sensitive that it could smell 1 molecule of skunk pong in 30 billion molecules of fresh air!

But you can't smell as well as a bloodhound. Their sense of smell is 1,000 times better than yours. But a wet bloodhound probably smells a thousand times worse than a wet you.

Look out!

Your eyes are like little cameras – but instead of film, the back of the eye has a sensitive surface called the retina. The image there appears upside down and your brain turns everything round the right way again.

Your retina has 137 million light-sensitive cells all crammed into an area smaller than a postage stamp. 130 million of these are for black and white vision and only 7 million are for colour. Yet you can still distinguish between 10,000 different colours.

About 1 in 30 people are colour blind, mostly men. Probably someone in your class at school is.

Blinking marvellous

Your eyelids keep your eyes clean by blinking. They blink about once every 6 seconds – that's about 10,000 times a day (they don't blink when you're asleep – just you look!).

Since each blink takes about 0.3 seconds, that means that even when you're awake your eyelids are shut for 50 minutes every day – that's nearly a fortnight every year. It better not be when you're on holiday!

Eerie ears

There are about 30,000 hair cells in your ears. When a noise makes them vibrate, we hear the noise.

Your ears can tell the difference between over 1,500 different tones of sound. That's 17 times more tones than there are on a piano.

Ears are full of sticky gungy wax. Its proper name is cerumen (bet your teacher won't know that). It oozes out of 2,000 glands within the ear and helps protect the very sensitive eardrum.

Noise is measured in decibels. The very lowest sound you can hear is 0 and the threshold of pain is 140. Beyond that it becomes too painful to listen and can damage your eardrum.

A rock concert can be over 100 decibels. A space rocket taking off can reach 190. If you really screamed out loud you might just reach 100 – but make sure everyone has ear plugs in first.

Waggle time

Do your ears waggle? Try it. There are muscles at the back of the ear that allow you to move them to and fro. What use is that? Not much – it's a leftover from our distant ape-like ancestors. These muscles allowed them to move their ears and pick up sounds better. Now they just help you move your glasses without touching them.

Canal trip

Ever taken a boat up a canal? Well, there are three canals in each of your ears, but you wouldn't get a boat in them. They're filled with a liquid that sploshes about when you move, and that tells your brain whether you're upside down or not. Your ears help you keep your balance.

The biggest ears in the world are those of the African elephant. They can each cover 2 sq m. It'd be like having a tablecloth on each side of your head. More likely to trip you up than help you balance!

Ears are also called lug-holes. 'Lug' is an old Scottish word for 'handle'. So watch out – your ears are just strong enough that you could still be picked up by them. Ouch!

The tiniest bone in your body is in the ear. It's called the stirrup bone and is about 2.5mm long. It's the same size when you're old as on the day you were born.

Hairy bits

Your hair is made of the same material that makes your finger- and toenails. It's called keratin and it's very strong.

There are 5 million hairs on your body. That's the same number as a gorilla has, but ours aren't as long or as thick.

The hairs on your head (there are about 100,000) grow about 13mm a month.

The longest known human hair was a beard that grew to 5.33m, which is almost as long as a giraffe is tall.

Fingernails grow about 0.3cm a month. The longest known fingernails belong to a man in India – they are 1.25m long. Imagine trying to eat or play with fingernails that long. And would it make it easier or more difficult to pick your nose?

Huffing and puffing

Your lungs are like huge wobbly wet curtains blowing in the wind. They're all folded up inside you, but if you unfolded them they'd cover 70 sq m.

Your lungs are full of tubes, called bronchi, which keep branching into smaller and smaller tubes, like the branches of a tree. If you could pull all these air-tubes out and lay them end to end, they'd stretch for 2,400km – all the way from London to Moscow.

Here are some numbers to take your breath away.

You breathe about 20 times a minute. (If you're a lazy so-and-so you might breathe only 12 times a minute – if you're rushing about it'll be up to 40 times a minute.)

That means you breathe 25,000 times a day, or about 680 million times in a lifetime.

With each breath, you suck in about 0.35 litres of air, along with 800,000 tiny bits of dust and dirt and muck. In a year you've breathed in enough air to fill 525,000 balloons – and created enough mucus to fill 30 bags of sugar.

It would take you 6 million breaths to fill a hot-air balloon – and that would take you about 8 months.

Pumping blood

Your heart is the most powerful organ in your body, yet it weighs only 300g.

• It beats about 100,000 times a day. In a lifetime it will beat over 3,000 million times, non-stop.

• It pumps about 4.7 litres of blood along 96,500km of rubbery tubing – your arteries and veins. That's equal to pumping it $2\frac{1}{2}$ times round the world.

Pongy poo

In your lifetime you'll probably eat about 50 tonnes of food. About 3 tonnes of that will come out the other end.

The entire human race produces a mound of poo equal to the size of the Great Pyramid in Egypt in less than 8 days.

In your lifetime you'll drink around 42,000 litres of liquid and most of that, about 27,000 litres, passes out again as urine.

The human race passes as much water in 1 day as flows over Niagara Falls in 18 minutes.

Belly aching

All that food and liquid and gas has passed a very long way through your body – in an adult the journey is over 8m, and can take 1 to 2 days.

It's a pretty straight route to the stomach where it sploshes about for 3 or 4 hours. Your stomach produces 2 litres of hydrochloric acid every day. This acid is so strong it could dissolve metal.

The stomach wall is lined with a sticky mucus to stop it being dissolved by the acid, and the whole stomach lining is replaced every 3 days at the rate of 500,000 cells a minute.

Your stomach turns all your food into a squidgy mush and this gets squeezed into the small intestine. This is 6m long – about as long as a drainpipe on a two-storey house, but it's only 4cm wide, so it's like a very long and very squidgy sausage.

The gungy slops are squeezed along here for 4 hours while your body takes all the goodness out of the food. The unwanted mush then plops into the large intestine. This is about 1.5m long – taller than you – and 6cm wide, so this really is like a drainpipe. Your food piles up here for a day or two ready for the toilet.

Windy woo

When you're eating and drinking – especially if you drink lots of fizzy pop – you gulp in lots of air. These gases whizz through the body in about 30 minutes and come out one end or the other!

Mindless mayhem

Are you frightened of snakes, spiders, homework? People are afraid of all kinds of things, and whatever it is there's a word for it.

What they call it	What you're frightened of
pogonophobia	beards (what would they make of a 5m one?)
paediphobia	children (maybe this isn't so strange!)
eosophobia	dawn (good reason to stay in bed)
pantophobia	everything (not much hope for them, sounds more like a morbid fear of knickers)
cherophobia	fun (must be a cheerful lot)
clinophobia	going to bed (because the bed-spider will get you)
microphobia	small objects (like teacher's brain)
emetophobia	vomiting (bet that makes them sick)
graphophobia	writing (any excuse not to do homework)

GET THIS!

The composer Arnold Schoenberg had triskaidekaphobia – he was afraid of the number 13. It turns out he was right to be too – he died aged 76 (7 + 6 = 13) on Friday 13 July 1951 at 13 minutes to midnight!

Dreaming

You dream every night, even if you don't remember it.

You start to dream after you've been asleep for about 90 minutes and will dream on and off all night. Most dreams last for less than 10 minutes, though they might seem to go on for hours.

In your lifetime you'll probably have 300,000 dreams – but how many will you remember?

Remember this!

Can you remember what you just read? This lot wouldn't have much trouble.

- Salo Finkelstein could remember 25 numbers chosen at random in any order having only glanced at them for a few seconds.
- Cardinal Mezzofanti could speak 53 languages fluently.
- Mehmed Ali Halici could recite 6,666 verses from the Koran from memory.
- Julius Tostee knew the entire Bible by heart.

How many facts can you remember?

Loads of children

The most children ever born to one mother is 69, to a Russian peasant, Madame Vassilyvev, who died in 1872.

We do not know the most children fathered by a single man, though Ismail as-Samin, Emperor of Morocco from 1672 to 1727, was reputed to have fathered at least 867 children.

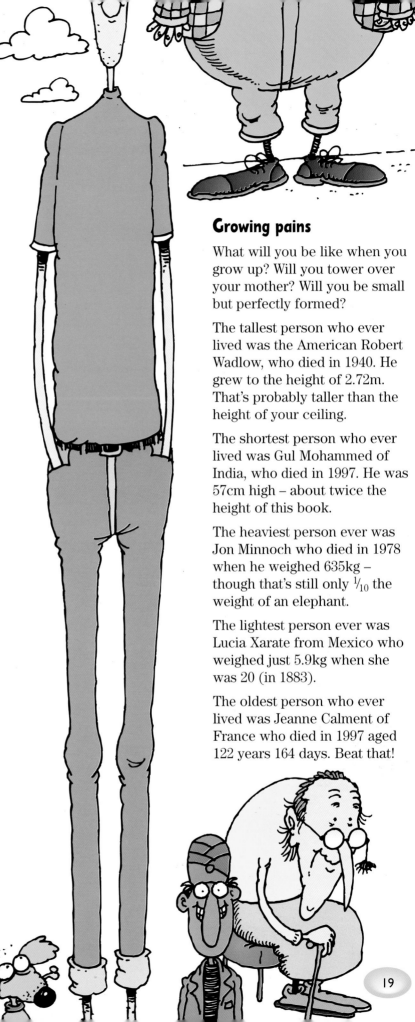

Growing pains

What will you be like when you grow up? Will you tower over your mother? Will you be small but perfectly formed?

The tallest person who ever lived was the American Robert Wadlow, who died in 1940. He grew to the height of 2.72m. That's probably taller than the height of your ceiling.

The shortest person who ever lived was Gul Mohammed of India, who died in 1997. He was 57cm high – about twice the height of this book.

The heaviest person ever was Jon Minnoch who died in 1978 when he weighed 635kg – though that's still only $\frac{1}{10}$ the weight of an elephant.

The lightest person ever was Lucia Xarate from Mexico who weighed just 5.9kg when she was 20 (in 1883).

The oldest person who ever lived was Jeanne Calment of France who died in 1997 aged 122 years 164 days. Beat that!

AMAZING ANIMALS AND STUPENDOUS PLANTS

Our planet is alive with creatures from the largest whales down to the tiniest, wriggliest little microbes. Scientists know of at least 2 million different species of animals and plants, but suspect there may be 3 times that out there still to be identified.

Someone with nothing better to do once worked out that there are 10 decillion living organisms on the Earth: that's

10,000,000,000,000,000,000,000, 000,000,000,000.

They could always be out by a few octillion.

Human beings account for about 6 billion of those. So let's ignore people and look at just a few of the other

9,999,999,999,999,999,999,999, 994,000,000,000

amazing creatures with which we share this planet.

Like . . .

- worms that could wrap themselves around the house you live in

- spiders as big as this book which can leap at you from trees
- plants older than the pyramids of Egypt
- beetles that are hundreds of times stronger than you

- frogs that kill
- and things that stink

Mind how you turn the page.

Biggest animal ever

The biggest animal living on Earth today is the blue whale. They can grow over 30m long and weigh more than 150 tonnes, making them larger than the biggest dinosaur (see page 36). One blue whale weighs more than 25 African elephants – or about the same as 2,400 teachers.

Even a newborn baby blue whale weighs about 7 tonnes. They grow at the rate of about 1 tonne every 10 days. How much do you weigh? Well a baby blue whale puts that much weight on every 7 to 8 hours!

And can that blue whale shout! It can make a sound louder than a jet engine (about 188 decibels). Because sound travels well under water, blue whales can be heard up to 800km away. It'd be like someone in London shouting to someone in Edinburgh.

Whopping wrigglers

Not as heavy as a whale but a lot more wriggly is the boot-lace worm. It lives in the mud under the sea and can grow up to 54m long.

The Australian gurgling worm can be as long as 3.7m and can be heard sucking and gurgling its way through the earth. It's the noisiest worm there is.

Because of its long tentacles the giant squid can be up to 18m long, while the Arctic giant jellyfish has tentacles that drift down into the sea for over 35m.

Slippery seaweeds

It's possible some seaweeds are 'taller' than the tallest trees. The giant kelp in the Pacific Ocean grows to lengths of 60m, and may grow up to 300m in colder waters. They are among the fastest growing plants, growing as much as 50cm each day. If you grew that fast, in 6 months you'd be as tall as the tallest tree.

The fastest growing land plant is bamboo. That grows up to 1m a day. So don't plant any under the bed.

GET THIS!

The largest fish ever captured was a whale shark in Thailand in 1919. It was 18m long, and weighed about 50 tonnes.

Heaviest — tallest — oldest ever trees

If you want to see something really big – and really old – go look in a forest.

In the Sequoia National Park, California, USA, is a Giant Sequoia called General Sherman. It's believed to be the largest living thing on Earth.

- It's 83.8m high
- It weighs about 2,200 tonnes – or more than 330 African elephants (or 35,000 teachers!)
- It's 25m around the trunk, so it'd take you and more than 20 friends linking hands to encircle the tree.
- It's believed to be about 3,500 years old, which means it was just starting to grow when Moses led the Israelites out of Egypt.
- It contains enough wood for 5 billion matchsticks.

The tallest ever tree was an Australian eucalyptus. Measured in 1872 it had grown to over 150m, but it has since fallen down.

The tallest *living* tree is a Douglas Fir in Oregon, which is 100m high.

The deepest known roots belong to the wild fig tree of South Africa, which go down over 120m.

Seriously old plants

The oldest plant in the world is believed to be a holly bush, *Lomatia tasmania*, that grows on Tasmania. Scientists believe it has been growing for 40,000 years. Its branches spread along the ground and some plant themselves so they look like a new tree. But it's just the one plant.

Other oldies are the bristlecone pines in America. The oldest living one is 4,600 years old, which means it started to grow when the pyramids were being built in Egypt, or when your great-great-great-great-great-great-great-great-great (+ another 170 greats) grandparents were alive (give or take a great)!

400 ft.

120 m.

23

Jumbo-sized

The African elephant is the largest living land animal. It's about 4m high and the biggest weigh up to 8 tonnes. They have the largest ears of any mammal – each is as big as a tablecloth. They also have the longest teeth – their tusks can be 2.7m long.

Tiniest ever

The smallest free-living organisms are bacteria, and the smallest is the *Pleuropneumonia* bacterium which is about 12 nanometres or 1/800,000th of a centimetre across.

It's impossible to imagine the number of bacteria on the Earth. Scientists have estimated there are about 5 nonillion of them

that's 5,000,000,000,000,000, 000,000,000,000,000.

There are about 50 million of them in the tiniest drop of liquid.

Bacteria divide on average once every 20 minutes. If all the cells survived, they would fill the entire Earth within less than 2 days (47 hours to be precise).

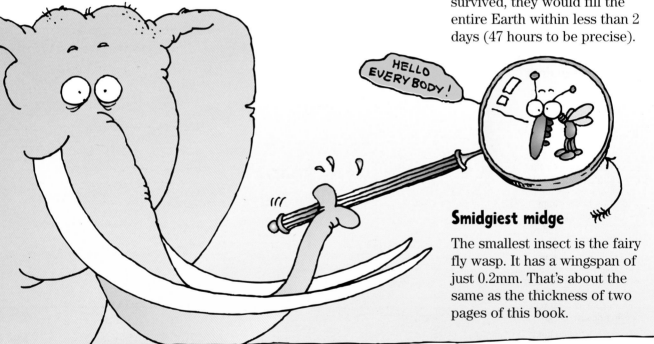

HELLO EVERYBODY!

Smidgiest midge

The smallest insect is the fairy fly wasp. It has a wingspan of just 0.2mm. That's about the same as the thickness of two pages of this book.

What a flap

The largest bird that can fly is the great bustard, which weighs up to 21kg. Its wingspan is about 2.7m. Pretty big, but not the biggest – the albatross has a wingspan of 3.6m. To get off the ground, the great heavy bustard has to run for ages and flap like mad.

Little flapper

The smallest bird is the Cuban bee hummingbird. It's 5.5cm long and weighs less than 2.5g. It lays the world's smallest eggs which are about the size of a pea.

Hummingbirds flap their wings faster than any other bird – an amazing 90 times a second.

Weeny weans

The newly born baby red kangaroo weighs only 28g and is 30,000 times smaller than its mother. If humans were like that you'd have been little bigger than an ant when you were born.

A trillion krillion

Bacteria are the most common living organisms, but they aren't classified as animals. The most common animal is the krill. They look like shrimps, and are 8–60mm long. There may be 600 trillion krill living in the world's oceans.

Krill are the main source of food for whales, and a single whale can eat 1 million krill in a single mouthful. That's the same as a whale eating 5,000 beefburgers in one go.

The most common land creatures are the insects. There are 1.2 quintillion insects on the Earth, which is 200 million insects for every person alive.

The most common insect is the termite. Termite nests can be as high as 6m and contain 2 million termites.

Some clever-clogs once estimated that the total weight of termites on the Earth was about 3 billion tonnes, or 9 times greater than the weight of all the human beings on the Earth!

Fishy pygmies

The world's smallest fish is the pygmy goby, which lives around coral reefs. It's no more than about 6mm long – smaller than your little fingernail.

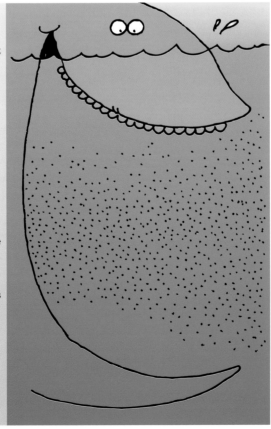

Greedy-guts

The greatest greedy-guts of all is the caterpillar of the polyphemus moth. It eats 86,000 times its own weight in just 48 hours. That would be like you eating 230 tonnes of food soon after you were born!

One locust can eat its own weight in food every day. An average swarm may contain 10 billion locusts and can consume 30,000 tonnes of food in 1 day. That's the same amount eaten by 10 million people (more than the population of London) in a day.

Camels can drink 113 litres of water in half an hour – nearly two baths full.

Snakes can swallow objects bigger than their heads. They disconnect their jaws and take in eggs and small mammals whole.

Vanishing fast

About 100 different species become extinct every day. More than 1,000 animal species are in danger of extinction.

There are only about . . .

5,000	Indian tigers left in the wild
2,000	black rhino
700	Giant pandas
250	Anatolian leopards
50	Asiatic cheetahs
11	Costa Rican golden toads
4	Californian condors

and there's only 1 Galapagos giant tortoise left, called Lonely George.

Speed merchants

The fastest a human has ever run is 40km/h. That's a dawdle in the animal world. Here are the real speed merchants.

	Animal	Speed
		km/h
fastest bird (diving)	peregrine falcon	298
fastest bird (flying)	spine-tailed swift	170
fastest mammal (running)	cheetah	112
fastest fish	sailfish	109
fastest mammal (swimming)	dolphin	64
fastest insect (flying)	Australian dragonfly	58
fastest bird (running)	ostrich	50
fastest reptile (running)	spiny-tailed iguana	35

No living thing flew faster than a falcon until 1919, when a man clocked a speed of 306km/h. Of course, the man was in an aircraft, which is cheating a bit.

Here are some other surprising animal speeds.

- a flying swan could overtake a cheetah at full pace
- a 2-day-old gazelle can outrun a full-grown horse
- an elephant can outrun the average human
- a penguin could match speed with a salmon
- a flying fish could keep pace with a flying swan
- the frigate bird can just outpace the flying fish. They can snatch the flying fish as they leap out of the water

Just picture an Olympic size swimming pool. One length of that pool is 50m, and the fastest any human has swum one length is 21.8 seconds. However:

- both a sea lion and a penguin would do it in 4.5 seconds
- a dolphin would do it in 2.8 seconds
- a blue shark would do it in 2.6 seconds
- a sailfish would do it in 1.6 seconds

World's greatest dawdlers

Of course not all animals are so fast.

The slowest of the slow are bacteria, which move at about 36cm per hour.

Of the big creatures, the three-toed sloth of South America moves (when it can be bothered) at about 110m per hour. Not that it would move for a whole hour. The sloth spends 80% of its life asleep, hanging upside down from trees. You may know someone like that.

Beetle power

You'd better not get hugged by a bug!

The world's biggest beetle is the Goliath beetle. It can cling so strongly to a branch that no one can pull it off.

The most weight lifted by a human is 2,844kg, about 40 times the average human body weight. That's nothing to the rhinoceros beetle. It can lift 100 times its own weight.

A dung beetle can push along balls of dung that are over 50 times its own weight. You would have to push the equivalent of three saloon cars at once to equal that.

Great bounders

How high or far can you jump? Of course, if it wasn't for your bad knee/ankle/foot, you'd be a record breaker, right?

The world high jump record for men is 2.45m, which is about 1.3 times the athlete's own height.

A flea can jump almost 20cm high – that's 130 times its own height. You'd have to jump 225m to equal that.

The tiny klipspringer antelope, which is only 50cm high, can leap 7.5m. To equal that, you would have to leap 28.5m, which would be like jumping in a single bound to the top of a church tower.

The world long jump record is 8.95m, which is about the same as a kangaroo can do in a single bound. The flea can jump up to 33cm or 220 times its body length. To do that you would have to leap 402m, which is as long as a queue of 120 cars.

Really ancient

Are your mum and dad really old? And what about your teachers? Absolutely ancient? Humans are surprisingly long-lived – you're likely to outlive most animals. Though you might just be beaten by a tortoise – they've been known to live for up to 116 years.

The longest-lived creatures are the lake sturgeon and the marine clam, both of which can live for up to 150 years.

In 1998, bacteria which had lived in bees 30 million years ago were recovered from amber, where the bees had been preserved. Scientists were able to grow these bacteria. The bacterial spores are now the longest-living organisms ever.

Was it worth it?

Adult mayflies live only just long enough to mate – usually only a few hours. Just imagine if you went through all the trouble of getting a girlfriend or boyfriend, then keeled over.

Incredible journeys

Birds fly tremendous distances.

The Arctic tern migrates every autumn all the way from the Arctic to the Antarctic, a journey of about 25,000km, and then, after a short rest, returns north in the spring.

The tiny ruby-throated hummingbird, which weighs only 3.5g, flies non-stop for 800km across the Gulf of Mexico from North to South America every autumn, returning the following spring.

Birds aren't the only animals to migrate. Every autumn grey whales migrate over 10,000km from the Arctic to their breeding grounds off the western coasts of Mexico. In the spring they make the return journey to the Arctic, this time with their baby calves.

TURN ONTO 170° FOR 16 MILES AT AN ALTITUDE OF 5,000 FT, THEN TURN ONTO 130° AND ASCEND TO 15,000 FT AND STAY ON THIS HEADING FOR 100 MILES.

Fantastic flights

The *most incredible migration of all* is that of the monarch butterfly.

Each spring a load of these butterflies (let's call them Flapper 1) leave their home in Mexico to fly north to Canada. They lay their eggs en route.

The butterflies that hatch from these eggs (Flapper 2) continue the journey to the Canadian border where they lay their eggs.

This new lot (Flapper 3) complete the journey far into Canada. During the summer a fourth generation of butterflies is born.

It's these butterflies (Flapper 4) that do the return trip to Mexico, in one journey, resting each night. The entire journey takes 3–4 weeks.

The longest trip known by one of these butterflies is 3,433km.

They arrive in vast swarms, usually in the exact same valley that their great-grandparents (Flapper 1) had left that spring.

But how do these butterflies know where to go, when they never knew their great-grandparents?

Spiny tails

Perhaps the weirdest migration is that of the spiny lobster. Every autumn they set off in groups of about 60 across the ocean floor between Florida and South America. They walk in single file, with each lobster holding on to the tail of the lobster in front. They walk about 16km a day.

Purr-sistence

The most incredible cat journey was made by Minosch, in 1981. He vanished from his owner's van when they stopped at the Turkish border on holiday. After 61 days, Minosch turned up at the family home on the island of Sylt in northern Germany, 2,400km away. He had travelled around 40km a day.

Busy bees

Next time you have a spoonful of honey just think what went in to making it.

One worker bee will gather 0.8g of honey during its entire short life of 35 days. It takes over 600 worker bees to gather enough honey for a 500g jar. To do that they'll have flown over 62,000km and visited over 2 million flowers.

In its lifetime a worker bee may fly as far as 20,290km, which is half way round the world.

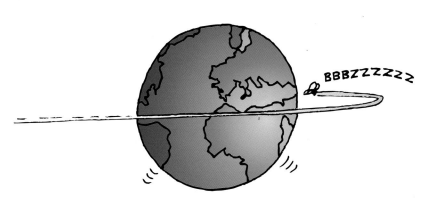

Creepy-crawlies

The creepiest crawly is the South African millipede, which has 710 legs (not 1000!) and can grow up to 35cm long.

The biggest millipede ever was the *Arthropleura*, which died out over 220 million years ago. It only had 45 pairs of legs but was about 1.8m long.

The biggest spider in the world is the South American Goliath bird spider. It would cover a page of this book. Its legs cover over 28cm and its body is 9cm long. It can weigh 122g, which is about the weight of an apple.

You could outrun most spiders but beware of the African sun spider. It can scuttle at over 16km/h.

The longest insect in the world is the tropical stick insect from Borneo. Its body is 32cm long.

The birdwing butterfly has the biggest wings of any insect. They're about 30cm across, which is about the same size as a pigeon's wings.

Instant death!

If you were bitten by the Australian taipan snake you'd be dead within minutes.

Almost as poisonous is the sea snake of the Timor Sea. One drop of venom could kill three people. It's 100 times more poisonous than the king cobra.

The poison of the sea wasp jellyfish can kill a person in under 3 minutes.

The golden arrow frog of South America oozes poison through its skin. One frog can produce enough poison to kill 1,500 people.

The most deadly fungus is the death cap, *Amanita phalloides*, often found around oak and beech trees. If eaten, it can kill within 6 hours.

Puffer fish are among the most poisonous of fish – the skin contains a toxin 25 times more dangerous than cyanide. Yet in Japan they are eaten as a delicacy. Although the poison is supposedly removed, at least 100 people die each year from eating them.

Stinky-pooh

The world's smelliest plant is the corpse lily, which smells like rotten meat. It uses the pong to attract flies which it eats.

The world's smelliest frog is the Venezuelan skunk frog, which lets off the same chemical used by the skunk. It's the pongiest smell in the world and you can detect it from over 1.6km away.

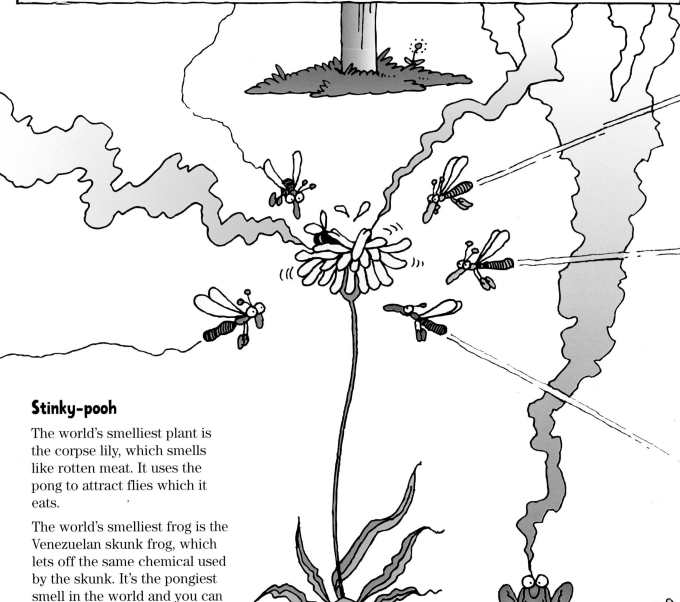

Super-dog

Is your best friend a dog?

In 1978, 5-year-old Kenny Homme fell into a creek which was flooded because of heavy rain. The water carried Kenny into a tunnel, where he would certainly have drowned, but at that point, the family dog, Chester, who had struggled through raging water for 10 minutes, reached Kenny. The boy was able to climb onto the dog's back and Chester brought him back to safety.

Extreme endurance

Hot stuff. Some bacteria can live in water at temperatures of 169°C. They live near vents of hot gas at the bottom of the sea and survive on sulphur rather than oxygen.

Cool customers. The African chironomid, an insect, can be frozen in liquid helium to –270°C, and still live when thawed out.

Cold feet

The record for cold endurance goes to the emperor penguin. Through the Antarctic winter, the male emperors gather together to incubate their eggs. They hold the egg on top of their feet to stop it freezing on the ice, enduring temperatures as low as –60°C and winds of up to 320km/h. They keep warm by huddling together and taking it in turns to stand on the outside.

Some mammals hibernate during the winter. All of their body processes slow down. The body temperature of the Arctic ground squirrel falls to below freezing (0°C) during hibernation.

When bats hibernate they may breathe only once every hour, and can go as long as 2 hours without breathing.

Darkest depths. The deepest part of the ocean is the Marianas Trench in the Pacific, which goes down for 11,022m. The pressure of water here is equal to 1 tonne pressing upon every square centimetre of your body. Yet near the bottom of this trench live sea pigs, a type of sea cucumber.

High there. Some bacteria drift in the Earth's atmosphere up to 41km, which is far into the stratosphere.

The highest a bird has flown is 11,280m. This was a vulture called the Rüppell's griffon. Unfortunately it collided with a plane.

Headless horrors. A cockroach can live for up to a week without a head.

Out numbered

A quarter of the world's bird species live in the Amazon forest.

All of the world's devil's-hold pupfish live in Nevada, USA – in fact they all live in the same pool. There are only about 200 of them.

There are 13 times more sheep in New Zealand than there are people.

There are over twice as many chickens in the world as people.

There has been life on Earth for millions and millions of years. Just think about all of the life on Earth today and then consider that it is only one-hundredth of all of the life that has ever lived.

Some of the biggest and fiercest creatures that ever lived were the dinosaurs, and they dominated this Earth for 160 million years.

It was a world of monsters – giant reptiles, giant flying creatures, giant trees and insects.

Here we'll look at the

- biggest
- fiercest
- fastest
- smartest
- smelliest
- and the most clumsy monsters that ever lived.

Time shrink

Let's first get to grips with the age of the Earth.

The Earth is 4,600 million years old and that is seriously old. It's millions of times older than both your grandparents and your teacher put together.

It is hard to imagine how old that is. So let's squeeze that 4,600 million years into just 1 year. Let's say Earth began on 1 January and we are now at midnight, on 31 December.

On that scale 1 second equals 146 years and just over 13 seconds have passed since the birth of Christ. Mankind has only been around for about 5 hours.

The dinosaurs first appeared around 15 December and were extinct 12 days later, or just 5 days ago!

In fact, if all of Earth's lifetime was converted to just 1 week instead of 1 year, then the dinosaurs died out 2½ minutes ago. They're actually our near neighbours in time, but humans would never have seen them. There were no humans (or hominids, as our ancestors are called) or teachers alive then.

Dinosaurs ruled the Earth for 160 million years. Mammals (including humans) have ruled the Earth for only about 60 million years, so there's still a long way to go.

In a way, dinosaurs are still with us. Birds are descended from one branch of dinosaurs – ever noticed how scaly the legs of a chicken are – and crocodiles are close relatives.

Slime-ball land

The very earliest life forms on Earth were bacteria that lived around hot volcanic springs about 3.8 billion years ago. The bacteria just waited for us to come along to give us colds and flu and other nasty things. But they had to wait a l-o-n-g time.

For the next 1.5 billion years, that was just about all the life there was – bacteria and algae. Earth was a world of slime!

Gunge world

During the next 2 billion years life got a bit more complicated but still didn't look much. By about 600 million years ago the most complicated life forms were ~~teachers~~, sorry, worms.

Hey, look here!

The first creatures with eyes were the trilobites, which lived about 550 to 250 million years ago. They couldn't see much, though, because they lived at the bottom of the sea. There were millions of them. They looked like a cross between a shrimp and a woodlouse. The biggest were up to 65cm long but most were about 1cm.

Bug bedlam

The first land creatures are still with us today – worms, snails, centipedes, millipedes and scorpions. It was from the centipede and millipede that all other insects evolved. The biggest of these creatures was the *Pterygotus* or 'water scorpion'. It grew up to 2m long.

For nearly 40 million years there was nothing on land but creepy-crawlies.

Some of the biggest insects lived about 300 million years ago. There were dragonflies with a wingspan of over 70cm whirring around the swamps like miniature planes.

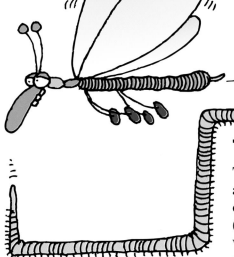

Fish tales

The first ancestor of the dinosaurs to appear on land was the *Ichthyostega*. It was a fish that could walk, and it waddled about on the land rather like a modern salamander. It lived about 370 million years ago.

The dinosaurs

There may have been as many as 1,500 different species of dinosaur. Palaeontologists (that's what they call scientists who study ancient life) are discovering a new species almost every month.

Not all of the dinosaurs lived at once. Each genus might have lived for between 5 and 20 million years before it either died out or evolved into something else. So an early dinosaur, like the giant plant-eating *Plateosaurus*, which lived around 200 million years ago, would never have known the *Tyrannosaurus*, which lived about 70 million years ago.

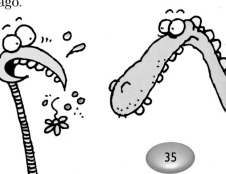

Mega monsters

The biggest dinosaurs of all weren't the most dangerous – unless they trod on you or thought you were a new species of tree. They were nearly all vegetarians and spent their time wallowing in lakes and rivers or swamps and munching leaves – a bit like us on holiday.

Most have been given BIG names like *Supersaurus*, *Ultrasaurus* or *Seismosaurus* (which means 'earth-shaking lizard'). One used to be called *Brontosaurus* (or 'thunder lizard') but isn't any more because it's the same as the *Apatosaurus*, which was found and named first. (*Apatosaurus* means 'deceptive lizard' – well, it certainly fooled them.) I much prefer *Brontosaurus* – bring back the *Brontosaurus*!

Here are the 10 most humungosaurus dinosaurs.

Dinosaur	Length m	Height m	Weight tonnes
Supersaurus	40	16.5	55–70
Argentinosaurus	40	15	80–100
Ultrasaurus	30.5	15	80–100
Seismosaurus	30	15	80–90
Diplodocus	27.5	14	11–15
Brachiosaurus	26	14	80–90
Barosaurus	25	10	15–20
Mamenchisaurus	22	14	11–15
Apatosaurus	21	12	30–35
Antarctosaurus	19	10	25–30

Daddy long-neck

Some dinosaurs had very long necks. The longest neck of any creature that has ever lived belonged to the *Mamenchisaurus*. It was 14m long. That's a long way to swallow. And just think – when it belched a burp must have come out like a cannon being fired.

Diplodocus had the longest tail – 15.2m. Its tail would still be entering your house while its head was going out the back.

Giant terrors

The biggest of the biggies may have been vegetarians, but the carnosaurs (meat-eaters) weren't exactly small.

Giganotosaurus was 6m tall, 14.3m long and weighed 8 tonnes.

Carcharodontosaurus was just a wee bit smaller – 5.7m tall, 13.5m long and weighing 8 tonnes.

The notorious *Tyrannosaurus rex* comes in third at 5.5m tall, 12.8m long and weighing 7 tonnes.

The big three were the most vicious hunters ever to prowl the Earth. However, they did not live at the same time. *Carcharodontosaurus* lived about 110 million years ago, *Gigantosaurus* about 90 million years ago and *Tyrannosaurus* – the quickest, most intelligent and deadliest of the three – about 70–65 million years ago.

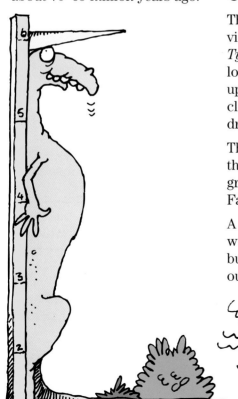

Sploshosaurus

There were also huge dinosaurs living in the sea. The *Elasmosaurus* could grow up to 15m. Half of its length was its neck, which it could raise up to 6m out of the water. Some people believe that a dinosaur like this is still around, living in Loch Ness in Scotland.

Crunchosaurus

The big three carnosaurs all had vicious teeth. The jaws of *Tyrannosaurus rex* were 1.2m long with 60 thick, sharp teeth up to 23cm long. Imagine cleaning those when they're dripping with flesh!

The *Edmontosaurus* had over a thousand teeth, used for grinding up thick vegetation. Fancy flossing those!

A dinosaur with a toothache would have been a real pain, but usually when a tooth fell out a new one grew.

Dimbosaurus

Some dinosaurs were probably extremely stupid. The *Stegosaurus*, which had a double set of bony plates along the ridge of its back, was 6m long but had a brain about the size of a walnut.

The huge *Zigongosaurus* was 11m long, weighed 20 tonnes and had a teeny tiny brain. It was probably the biggest, thickest dinosaur of all.

Some dinosaurs were too big for their own good. If they were bitten in the tail it took a second or two before their brain realized it. The *Zigongosaurus* may already have been half-eaten before it cottoned on!

Smartie-osaurus

There were some dinosaurs that did have something between their ears, though.

The brainiest dinosaurs were the raptors. They were cunning, fast and very dangerous. Never play with a velociraptor. It'd cheat – then eat you.

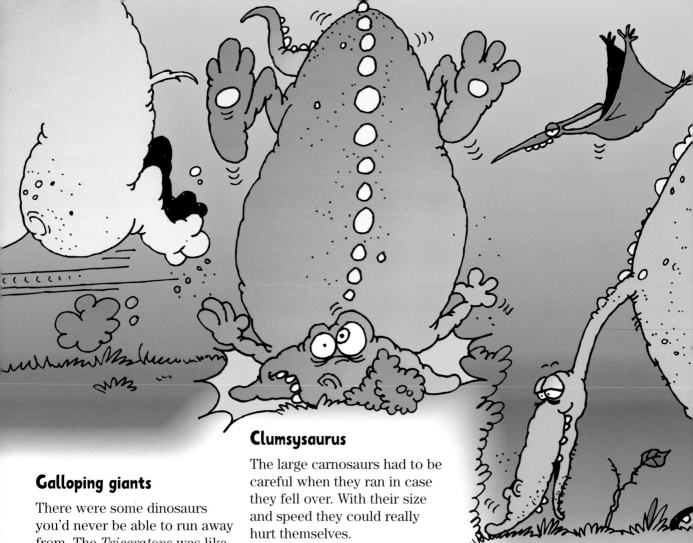

Galloping giants

There were some dinosaurs you'd never be able to run away from. The *Triceratops* was like a rhinoceros and could reach speeds of up to 50km/h. That's faster than an African elephant, though they both weigh about 6 tonnes.

Even the mighty *Tyrannosaurus* could run at least 30km/h.

The fastest dinosaurs were the small bird-like ones. Both *Ornithomimus* and *Struthiomimus* looked rather like an ostrich without its feathers, and could reach speeds of 60–70km/h.

Almost as quick were the raptors, and they were smaller and more nimble. The velociraptors would make the best football team – except they'd probably eat the referee and run off with the football.

Clumsysaurus

The large carnosaurs had to be careful when they ran in case they fell over. With their size and speed they could really hurt themselves.

Judging from broken bones found among fossils, the most clumsy dinosaur was the *Allosaurus*. It probably kept running into trees and falling over logs as it rushed to catch its next meal. You know the type.

Pretty baby

Not all dinosaurs were big. The *Compsognathus* (which means 'pretty jaw') was only about 75cm long, half of which was its long, thin tail, and it weighed about the same as a large chicken (about 2.7kg). It was a meat-eater and an efficient killer judging from its very sharp teeth, despite its size.

This dinosaur may well have been the ancestor of the birds.

Flying terrors

The earliest known bird was the *Archeopteryx*. It had feathers and was about the size of a crow, but it also had teeth and otherwise looked like a small dinosaur. It lived about 160 million years ago.

The *Pteranodon* had a wingspan of about 7m and had a large horn jutting back along its head which probably created a whistling or roaring sound as it flew, a bit like a flying kettle.

The biggest dinosaur that could fly was the *Quetzalcoatlus*. It had a wingspan of up to 15m and would have looked like a glider.

Stenchosaurus

Because of the vegetation they ate and their poor digestion, it's believed that many dinosaurs would have let off lots of wind.

The worst may well have been *Ankylosaurus* – stinkylosaurus more like it! It had a large gut where food fermented, so it must have popped all day long.

The world of dinosaurs was probably filled with growling, belching and ripping noises, and must have stunk like mad. And what happened to all the dino-pooh?

Gone with the wind

There is a theory that because these huge plant-eating dinosaurs let off so much wind, this led to a build-up of methane gas in the atmosphere and the dinosaurs gassed themselves to death.

A more probable but far less funny theory is that a huge meteor struck the Earth and set off a series of major volcanic eruptions. Millions of tonnes of dust and debris were thrown up into the atmosphere, cooling the planet and causing acid rain.

Scientists have estimated that the impact of the meteor was equal to a megaton bomb being detonated over every square kilometre of the Earth's surface.

All land animals weighing more than about 25kg died out. It took millions of years for life to recover.

That's how mammals inherited the Earth.

Out of Africa

Your distant ancestors appeared in Africa about 5 million years ago (about 9 hours ago in our Earth year). They were the australopithecines. This means 'southern ape'. It doesn't mean they came from Australia or hopped like a kangaroo.

After 3 million years their descendants, *Homo habilis* ('handy man') mastered fire and learned to use stone tools. They probably soon mastered the drums, but the guitar and keyboards took another 2 million years.

They became more upright and so we call them 'upright man' or *Homo erectus*. Over thousands of years their intelligence grew and they became 'wise man' or *Homo sapiens* – but they still hadn't invented the guitar. In fact they hadn't even invented the wheel, so still had to walk to work.

Homo sapiens were originally hunter-gatherers, but as the Ice Age retreated they turned to farming the land. The first towns and cities began to appear about 10,000 years ago – the last minute in our Earth year.

Lost monsters

The world of *Homo erectus* and early *Homo sapiens* was similar to ours today, but with some differences. Although the dinosaurs had long gone there were still other giant creatures.

The *Megatherium* was a giant sloth that looked like a huge bear. It was about 6m long and 3m high at the shoulder.

The *Mammuthus* was a large woolly mammoth, bigger than an elephant, standing about 4m high.

The *Aepyornis* or elephant bird was the biggest bird that ever lived. It looked like a giant ostrich, stood up to 3m tall and weighed 450kg. Thankfully for humans, it could not fly.

Aepyornis laid the biggest eggs ever. They were 86cm long, 72cm round, and weighed 12.2kg. They were seven times bigger than an ostrich's egg, and held nearly 11 litres – imagine what a huge omelette that would have made.

The *Smilodon* was a large sabre-toothed cat about 2m long. It had large upper canine teeth, up to 15cm long. What a smile that would be!

All of these creatures died out about 10,000 years ago, but your ancestors would have known them.

Gone for ever

Animals continue to die out, even within recent history. The best known example was the dodo – we say 'as dead as a dodo' when something's well and truly dead. The dodo was an ungainly flightless bird that lived on the island of Mauritius. The last one died in about 1681.

The Barbary lion was the creature that the Romans once let loose on the Christians in the arena. They used to live in North Africa, but the last one was shot in 1922.

The New Zealand moa, a flightless bird up to 3.5m tall, was extinct by about 1850.

Hundreds of other species of animals have died out in the last few centuries, and it's getting worse. You'll find more about animals and birds that are threatened with extinction on page 25.

Middle age

It is just possible that some creatures we thought had died out still survive in remote parts of the world. Some of these mystery creatures are covered on pages 74–79.

Life on Earth today is the product of 3,800 million years of evolution. But the Earth is still only approaching middle age. There are at least another 4,000 million years before the Sun becomes too hot to support life on Earth. That means life is only halfway through its evolution (maybe a bit less for maths teachers).

Just think what other life forms might develop in the future! They could be even more incredible than the dinosaurs.

Super stars

The most stars you can see in one go, without a telescope, is about 2,500 – but that's nothing compared with the total number of stars in the Universe.

Our solar system is just a small part of one galaxy, which we call the Milky Way. Our galaxy contains about 100 billion stars. If each star were the size of a grain of rice, this number would fill a cathedral.

In total there are estimated to be around 100 billion galaxies, each with about the same number of stars. That's a total of 10 sextillion stars or 10,000,000,000,000,000,000,000. And that's probably on the low side!

Nearest star

The nearest star to Earth is our Sun. It's about 150 million km away. Light from the Sun takes 8 minutes 19 seconds to reach us.

The next nearest star is Proxima Centauri which is so far away that light takes 4.25 years to reach us – so we say it is 4.25 light-years away.

GET THIS!

The greatest speed possible is the speed of light. It travels at 300,000km per second. A light-year is the distance light travels in 1 year. This is equal to 9,458,688 million km.

If you could fly into space directly by Concorde, it would take 7.3 years to get to the Sun, but it would take nearly 2 million years to reach Proxima Centauri.

Most distant stars

The furthest known stars from the Earth are in the remotest known galaxy of all. The galaxy doesn't yet have a name, and was only discovered in 1997. The light reaching us from these stars left them 13 billion years ago, which was soon after the Universe was created, and long before the Earth was formed.

Biggest and brightest

The brightest star you can see in the night sky is Sirius. It is about 26 times brighter than the Sun, but appears less bright because it is further away. As stars go, it's actually quite close, about 8.64 light-years. You can find Sirius by looking at the constellation of Orion and following the belt of Orion down to the left.

The brightest known star in our galaxy is Eta Carinae, which is as bright as 6 million of our Suns. It's about 6,400 light-years away. About 100 years ago it was one of the brightest stars in the sky, but since then it has become surrounded by space dust and is now hidden from the naked eye.

Can you see it?

The biggest star you can see in the sky is Betelgeuse (pronounced 'bet-el-jeuz'). You'll find it in the top left corner of Orion. Betelgeuse has a diameter of 1 billion km, which is 718 times wider than our Sun.

Miles and miles away

Everything about the Universe is massive and everything in it is a long way away.

Mercury is closer to the Sun than we are, but it's still 57.9 million km from it, and light from the Sun takes 3 minutes to reach it.

Pluto, the most distant planet from the Sun, is 5,913.5 million km away. The Sun's light takes 5.5 hours to get there.

That's a mere hop and a skip compared with the distance from the Sun to the Oort Cloud (home of the distant comets). It takes 577 days for the Sun's light to reach the Oort Cloud, which is 15 trillion km away.

But say you leapt into the fastest spaceship there is and zoomed off beyond our solar system. How long would it take you to reach some of those fantastic stars, going at a cool 112km per second?

	Distance in Light-years	How long to get there (years)
Proxima Centauri	4.25	18,000
Sirius	8.64	37,000
Betelgeuse	650	2.78 million
Eta Carinae	6,400	27.3 million
Nearest galaxy	80,000	213 million
Furthest you can see without a telescope (the Andromeda Spiral)	2,200,000	9.4 billion
Furthest known galaxy	13,000,000,000	55.5 trillion
Edge of Universe	Over 14,000,000,000	60 trillion

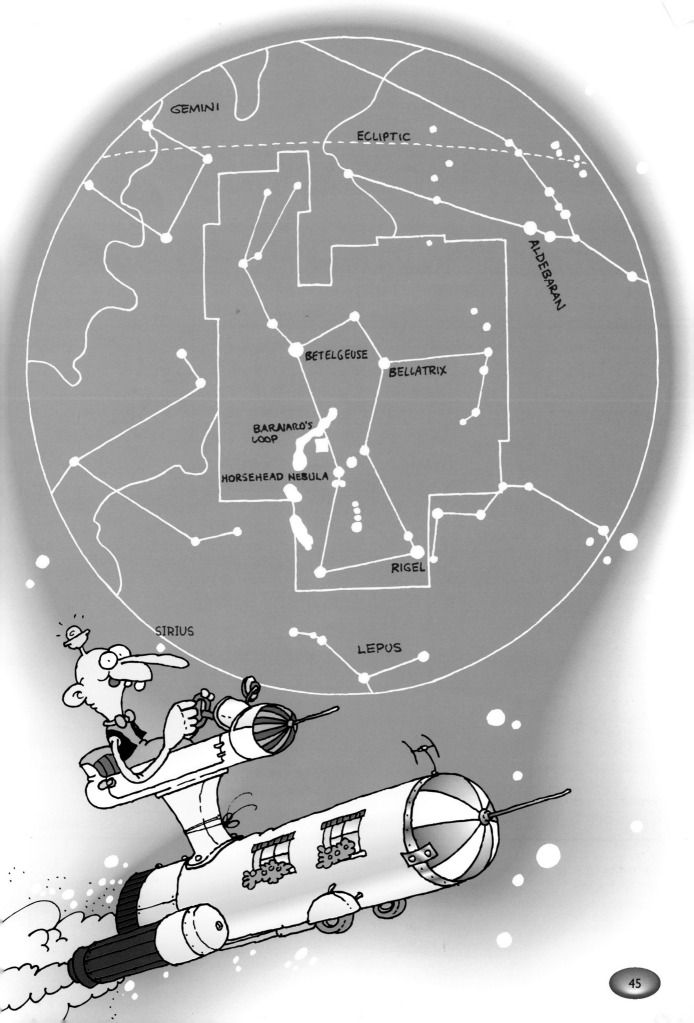

Stupendous speed

Speed in space is awesome. Remember that space is virtually a vacuum so there's nothing to stop objects moving at a high speed.

GET THIS!

You may think you're sitting still, but really you're moving at a terrific speed. The Earth is spinning on its axis at 1,670km/h. The Earth is moving around the Sun at 107,160km/h. And then we are moving with the Sun around the centre of the galaxy at 792,000km/h.

Shooting stars

The fastest objects you'll normally see are meteoroids when they strike the Earth's atmosphere and burn up (they're called shooting stars). They are travelling at about 60km per second.

Comets can reach even more awesome speeds. The fastest comet yet seen was discovered in 1996 and given the unglamorous name of C/1996 S3 Soho. It was a Sun-grazer, meaning it swings very close by the Sun. It reached the phenomenal speed of 618km per second.

All planets are actually falling towards the Sun, but are stopped from falling into the Sun by their speed in orbit. Mercury travels at a cosmic 172,332km/h (nearly 48km per second!).

Dawn of time

The Universe is believed to be between 14 and 15 billion years old. The age of our own solar system is estimated to be about 4.6 billion years. The Sun's total lifetime is reckoned to be about 11 billion years. So the solar system is only just approaching middle age.

Dead stars and black holes

Stars do eventually die. They burn off all their fuel leaving behind an extremely dense core called a neutron star. If the star was big, the core may have a pull of gravity so great that light cannot escape from it. When this happens it becomes a black hole. A black hole is not really a hole, but a point of super-gravity from which nothing can escape.

Black holes are the most dangerous places in the Universe. If you get too close to one you'll be crushed right out of existence.

You may have heard of the Big Bang. It's how most scientists think the Universe began. The Big Bang wasn't like an explosion, but was a sudden expansion, as if a balloon was being inflated at a terrific speed.

The Universe may come to an end one day, and maybe all that will be left is a black hole from which a new Universe may one day erupt, just like our own did with the Big Bang. But don't worry, this won't happen for billions and billions of years.

Sunny and bright

The Sun is a star. You should never look directly at it because it is so bright it could damage your eyes, even if you are wearing sunglasses. It is 600,000 times brighter than the full Moon.

The Sun is a massive ball of hot gas. It's the most massive object in the solar system by far – you could fit 1,303,600 Earths inside it. In fact it contains 99.8% of the total mass of the solar system.

The pressure at the centre of the Sun is immense. It is about 10 billion times the surface pressure on Earth.

The temperature on the 'surface' of the Sun (the visible area we see) is a cool 5,500°C. Some parts of the surface are even cooler, about 4,000°C, and these look darker and are called sunspots. Some sunspots are huge – as much as 100,000km wide, or 8 times the diameter of the Earth.

Above the visible surface it's even hotter, and in the corona (the Sun's atmosphere, which you see during a total eclipse of the Sun), the temperature is as high as 2 million°C.

The temperature at the centre of the Sun is an incredible 15 million°C.

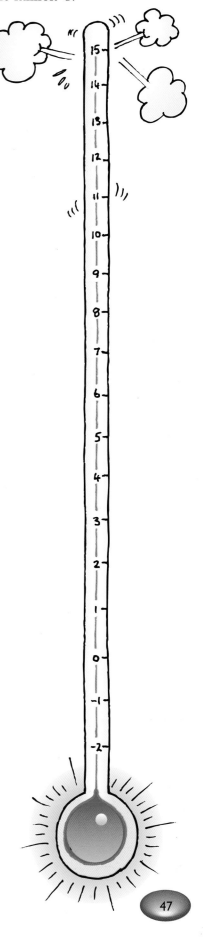

Full Moon

Astronomers believe that the Moon was created when a massive object hit the Earth when it was still forming and threw a huge chunk of molten rock into space where it cooled and became the Moon.

The Moon always presents the same face to the Earth. No one knew what the other side of the Moon looked like until the Russian spacecraft *Luna 3* sent back photographs in 1959.

The Moon is one of the slowest objects in the solar system. It travels only 1.6 times faster than Concorde.

The Moon has no atmosphere. So everything that happens on the Moon, even the impact of a meteorite, happens in complete silence. There are no winds, so everything on the Moon's surface remains undisturbed unless bombarded from space. The footprints left by the astronauts who walked on the Moon over 30 years ago are still there.

The temperature on the Moon's surface varies from 117°C at noon to −163°C at night. No human could survive those extremes.

THE PLANETS

The Earth is just one of nine major planets known to orbit the Sun. Let's have a look at some of the others.

Mercury

Mercury is the closest planet to the Sun. It has the most extreme temperatures of any planet, ranging from 427°C by day to −183°C at night.

Mercury has a very long day, which lasts for 59 Earth days – your Mum could not say 'there just are not enough hours in a day!' if she lived on Mercury.

Mercury's surface is pitted with craters like the Moon. It has no life, there is no sound, and little has changed on the surface for over 3,000 million years.

Venus

Venus is surrounded by dense poisonous clouds. No one knew what the surface looked like until pictures were sent back by the Russian space probe *Venera 9* in 1975.

Venus is the hottest planet in the solar system. The temperature on the surface is always about 460°C.

The intense heat, the suffocating air pressure, and the burning acid rain make the surface of Venus the most hostile place in the solar system, so don't book any holidays there.

A day on Venus is equal to 243 Earth days. Because Venus orbits the Sun in 225 days it means its day is longer than its year.

Mars

Mars is known as the Red Planet – its surface is rich in rusted iron, which makes it look red.

Mars has the largest volcano so far found in the solar system, called Olympus Mons. It is 24km high – 3 times higher than Mount Everest.

Mars has an atmosphere, but it's almost all carbon dioxide.

There is no liquid water on the surface, but there is ice at the poles.

The surface temperature ranges from 26°C in the day to as low as –110°C at night, so the average temperature is always below freezing. It's like a permanent Arctic.

Mars has two tiny moons – Phobos and Deimos. Phobos is so small, that in just over a kilometre you could walk from the day side where the temperature is like a winter's day in Scotland (about –4°C) to the night side, which is like Antarctica (–122°C).

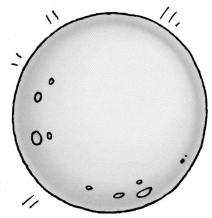

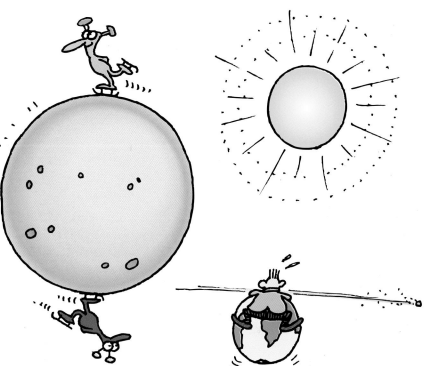

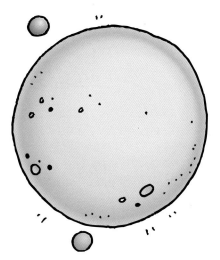

Asteroids

These are lumps of rock that orbit the Sun, mostly between Mars and Jupiter.

There may be as many as 100,000 asteroids, most of them only a few metres in diameter. There are only about 50 with diameters more than 160km.

The biggest is Ceres, with a diameter of 940km.

Earth-grazers

Some asteroids pass close to the Earth and are called Earth-grazers. One of them came within 104,000km in 1994. Although it was not much more than 6m wide, it would have caused widespread devastation if it had hit the Earth.

Rocks have hit the Earth in the past. The most recent collision was at Tunguska in Siberia in 1908. It hit the Earth with the power of a large hydrogen bomb and devastated an area 80km across.

Jupiter

Jupiter is the biggest planet in the solar system. It could swallow over 1,300 Earths – in fact it's bigger than all the other planets put together, twice over!

Jupiter is a gas giant – most of the planet is made up of gas, not rock like the Earth. It has a small rocky core, surrounded by a vast ocean of liquid hydrogen, thousands and thousands of kilometres deep.

The atmosphere on Jupiter stinks. It is made up of ice crystals of ammonia, methane and water.

The best known feature in Jupiter's atmosphere is called the Great Red Spot, which isn't named after your zits! It's probably the vortex of a giant hurricane about the same size as the Earth. This storm has been raging for at least the last 350 years.

Jupiter has 16 moons. One of them, Io, is covered by volcanoes that are constantly erupting. The lava from these volcanoes is hotter than anything in the solar system outside the Sun. It reaches temperatures of up to 1,700°C. Yet away from these volcanoes the temperature remains far below freezing.

GET THIS!

Titan is the likeliest place in our solar system, outside Earth, for life to develop. The surface is bitterly cold (about –170°C), but it could be that in millions of years, when our Sun grows old, the extra heat given out (which will destroy the Earth) might help life develop on Titan.

Saturn

Saturn is the second largest planet, and another gas giant. It is far less dense than Jupiter, and would in fact float on water (if you could find enough!).

Saturn is renowned for its rings. They are made up of millions of tiny rocks, some as small as grains of sand, but others as large as 10m across.

It has at least 18 moons. One of them, Titan, is the second largest moon in the solar system.

Uranus

Uranus is unusual in two ways. It is tipped over on its side, so it rolls around in orbit. Also, it spins the opposite way round to all the other planets.

Uranus is a gas giant like Jupiter but is much smaller – though it is still as big as 67 Earths. Its atmosphere is thick in methane, so it stinks too.

Pluto

Pluto is the furthest planet known. It was not discovered until 1930.

Pluto is so distant that it takes 248 Earth years to orbit the Sun once. That means it hasn't done one complete orbit since it was discovered.

Pluto is the smallest planet, and is even smaller than our own Moon. Some astronomers think it is too small to be a proper planet but is simply a large asteroid.

Pluto is the coldest planet in the solar system with a temperature of about –230°C.

Neptune

Neptune, another gas giant, is almost the same size as Uranus.

Its atmosphere is torn apart by the strongest winds in the solar system, blowing at up to 2,200km/h – about as fast as Concorde flies.

Comets

Far out in the depths of space beyond Pluto's orbit is the home of the comets. Maybe as many as 200 billion small rocks and planetoids orbit the Sun out there. Occasionally these rocks are dislodged from their orbit, spiral in towards the Sun, and become comets.

Comets are huge chunks of rock covered in ice. As they approach the Sun the ice melts and turns into gas. This streams out behind the comet creating the comet's tail. Although a comet is usually not more than a few kilometres in diameter, the tail can stretch out for over 150 million km.

The best known is Halley's comet which comes near to the Earth every 76 years. It was last here in 1986 and will return in 2062. Halley's comet loses about 14,000kg of ice every second, that's about 300kg every visit.

Into the infinite

Scientists have detected planets around other distant stars. The chances are that somewhere out there, there are planets like Earth that may also support life. The search for extra-terrestrial life continues, but will we ever find any – or will they find us first!?

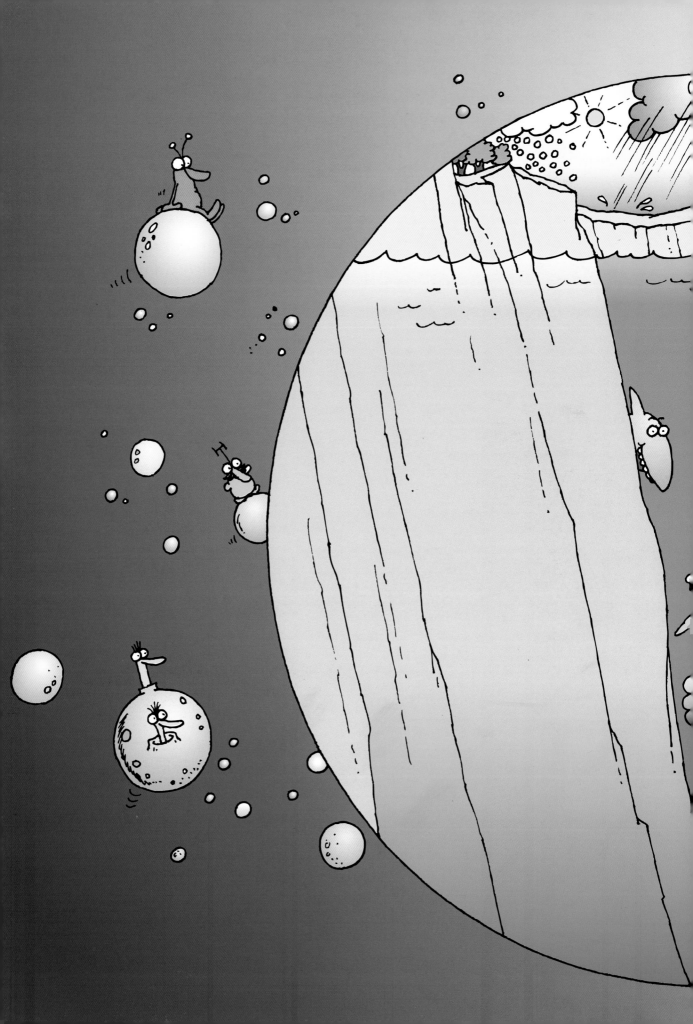

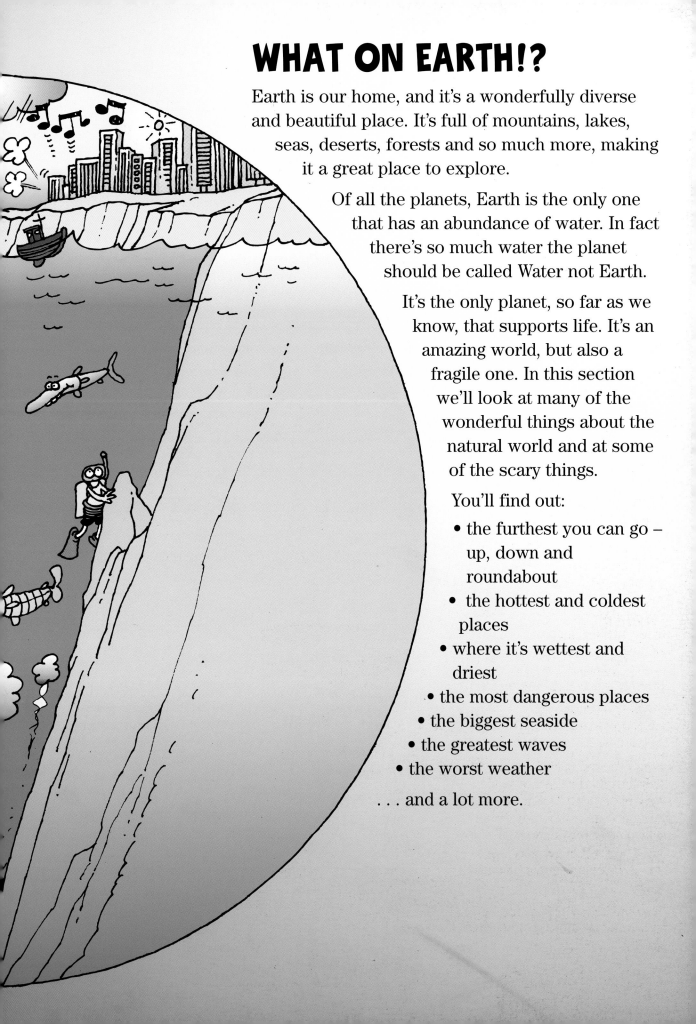

WHAT ON EARTH!?

Earth is our home, and it's a wonderfully diverse and beautiful place. It's full of mountains, lakes, seas, deserts, forests and so much more, making it a great place to explore.

Of all the planets, Earth is the only one that has an abundance of water. In fact there's so much water the planet should be called Water not Earth.

It's the only planet, so far as we know, that supports life. It's an amazing world, but also a fragile one. In this section we'll look at many of the wonderful things about the natural world and at some of the scary things.

You'll find out:

- the furthest you can go – up, down and roundabout
- the hottest and coldest places
- where it's wettest and driest
- the most dangerous places
- the biggest seaside
- the greatest waves
- the worst weather

. . . and a lot more.

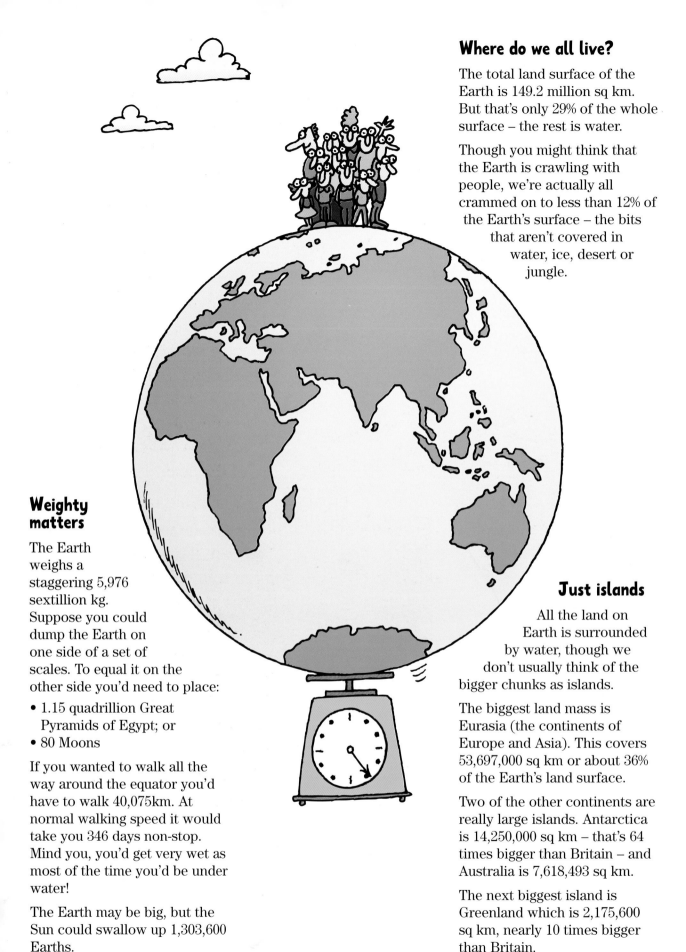

Where do we all live?

The total land surface of the Earth is 149.2 million sq km. But that's only 29% of the whole surface – the rest is water.

Though you might think that the Earth is crawling with people, we're actually all crammed on to less than 12% of the Earth's surface – the bits that aren't covered in water, ice, desert or jungle.

Weighty matters

The Earth weighs a staggering 5,976 sextillion kg. Suppose you could dump the Earth on one side of a set of scales. To equal it on the other side you'd need to place:

- 1.15 quadrillion Great Pyramids of Egypt; or
- 80 Moons

If you wanted to walk all the way around the equator you'd have to walk 40,075km. At normal walking speed it would take you 346 days non-stop. Mind you, you'd get very wet as most of the time you'd be under water!

The Earth may be big, but the Sun could swallow up 1,303,600 Earths.

Just islands

All the land on Earth is surrounded by water, though we don't usually think of the bigger chunks as islands.

The biggest land mass is Eurasia (the continents of Europe and Asia). This covers 53,697,000 sq km or about 36% of the Earth's land surface.

Two of the other continents are really large islands. Antarctica is 14,250,000 sq km – that's 64 times bigger than Britain – and Australia is 7,618,493 sq km.

The next biggest island is Greenland which is 2,175,600 sq km, nearly 10 times bigger than Britain.

Beside the seaside

The total length of the coastline around all the continents and islands in the world is 848,000km. This is further than the distance from the Earth to the Moon and back again.

The longest coastline of any country is Canada's, which is 243,791km long. Unfortunately, much of it is frozen for most of the year, so it's not a good place for a long-distance paddle.

The country with the shortest coastline is Monaco, which is less than 4km, but it's also the richest, with millions of pounds worth of yachts moored there.

Cliffs and canyons

The island of Molokai, in Hawaii, has cliffs over 1,005m high. They're nearly 6 times higher than the famous cliffs at Beachy Head on the English south coast.

The Grand Canyon in Arizona is the largest chasm in the world. It is

• over 349km long
• up to 20km wide
• down to 2,133m deep.

Although not as long as the Grand Canyon, Hell's Canyon in Oregon and Idaho is the deepest. The Snake River flows 2400m below the towering cliffs of Devil Mountain.

Far away from anywhere

The most remote island in the world is Bouvet Island. No one lives here. It's 1,700km from the nearest neighbour, which is also uninhabited – Antarctica. The nearest people are over 2,000km away on the tiny island of Tristan da Cunha, which is the most remote island where people live.

— GET THIS! —

The most populated and noisiest island in the world is Hong Kong. Not the place for getting away from it all!

Gigantic waves

Ordinary waves are caused by the wind. The highest natural wave ever spotted was 34m from trough to crest. This was in the Pacific Ocean during a hurricane in 1933.

Earthquakes or volcanic explosions also cause waves. These are called tsunamis. The highest recorded tsunami was 85m high, or twice the height of Nelson's Column. The fastest recorded tsunami was travelling at 900km/h.

— GET THIS! —

In 1868 a tsunami over 15m high struck the island of Minole in Hawaii. In order to save his life, a Hawaiian called Holua, rode the wave on a surfboard!

How far down can you go?

The deepest ocean is the Pacific. At its deepest point it goes down to 11,022m. This is in the Marianas Trench near the island of Guam. This trench is so deep it would swallow Mount Everest.

The Marianas Trench is far deeper than the deepest known caves which are the Reseau Jean Bernard in France. They only go down 1,602m.

Humans have drilled deeper than this. The deepest borehole is on the Kola Peninsula in Russia where geologists have drilled 12km into the Earth's crust. That's as if they'd drilled from the very top of Everest to the very bottom and half way up again.

Under your feet

What is under the surface of the Earth?

The distance to the centre of the Earth is about 6,360km, which is about the same as the distance across the United States from New York to Los Angeles. It doesn't seem very far, but the journey would be hard to make, solid in fact.

First you'd have to get through the Earth's crust. This is solid rock between 5 and 35km thick.

If the Earth were the size of an apple, the crust would be equal to the apple's skin.

Below the crust is the Earth's mantle. The further down you go the hotter it gets. The rocks start to turn to jelly and then melt into liquid rock, the same as lava that spews out of volcanoes.

At a depth of 5,000km, you enter the Earth's core. Here the temperature is 6,000°C. That's hotter than the surface of the Sun.

Highest heights

How far can you go up and still be on land?

Mount Everest (also called Chumulongma) at 8,846m is usually called the highest mountain in the world. But it isn't! It's the highest point above sea level.

The tallest mountain in the world is Mauna Kea, a Hawaiian volcano that measures 10,206m from bottom to top. However, $\frac{3}{5}$ of it (6,000m) are under water. It's as high as almost 27 Empire State Buildings or 181 Nelson's Columns.

Soggiest mountains

The highest mountain that is totally covered by water is an unnamed peak in the Tonga Trench just south of Tonga in the Pacific. It is 8,690m high, and its peak is 365m below the surface of the sea.

The world's longest mountain range is entirely under water. It runs all the way down the centre of the Atlantic Ocean and is called the Mid-Atlantic Ridge. It's 11,300km long, which is much longer than the longest mountain range on land. This is the Andes in South America, which is 7,242km long.

Drifting continents

Believe it or not the continents are still moving at about 3cm a year – or 12 times slower than your fingernails grow. Over 65 million years this is equal to 1,950km!

Making mountains

Mountains are formed by upward movements and folding of the Earth's rocky crust. This happens because the continents are still moving. When India bumped into Asia the land inbetween buckled and the Himalayas were formed.

— GET THIS! —

Where is the furthest and closest point from the centre of the Earth? Because the Earth spins, it bulges at the equator and is slightly flatter at the poles.

Droughting deserts

We think of deserts as hot, dry, sandy places, but a desert is any waste land where scarcely anything grows. The world's biggest desert is the Antarctic. 98% of its surface is permanently covered with ice. The rest is barren rock.

─ GET THIS! ─

The ice on Antarctica is up to 4.7km thick and weighs 25.2 quintillion kg. If all that ice melted, the sea levels would rise everywhere in the world by about 200m. That's enough to bury the British Telecom Tower in London.

The largest hot desert is the Sahara in North Africa. It covers 8,400,000 sq km – it's about 16 times the size of France.

The driest desert in the world is the Atacama in Chile, South America – there are parts where it hasn't rained for hundreds of years. So remember to take a drink with you.

Exploding mountains

When a volcano explodes it throws ash, rocks and dust into the sky. Molten rock (called lava) spurts out and flows down the mountain side like a red-hot river.

The world's highest volcano is Aconcagua in the Andes. It is 6,960m high, but has not erupted for millions of years.

The highest active volcano is Guallatiri, in Chile, which is 6,060m high. The last time it erupted was in 1959.

The most famous volcano is probably Mount Vesuvius in Italy. In AD 79 it erupted, and the lava buried the towns of Pompeii and Herculaneum in mud and rocks over 18m deep. Vesuvius is one of the world's most dangerous volcanoes, because so many people live near it.

The biggest bangs

The loudest volcanic eruption of recent times happened in Indonesia on the island of Krakatoa in 1883. The explosion hurled rocks 55km into the air. The sound of it was heard up to 4,800km away. The eruption caused a tidal wave over 41m high.

Edinburgh Castle is built on the core of an extinct volcano.

The island of Surtsey suddenly appeared in 1963 off the coast of Iceland. It was formed by an undersea volcano.

The eruption of Santorini on the island of Thira in the Aegean Sea, near Greece, in 1470 BC destroyed the civilization of Crete. It left behind beaches of black ash – imagine playing on a beach of coal dust. I bet it gets pretty hot in the sun.

Shuddering shocks

Earthquakes happen when pressures build up and cause the Earth's crust to suddenly buckle and shift. Most earthquakes last for only a second or two, but the San Francisco earthquake of 1906 lasted for 47 seconds.

There are half a million earthquakes a year, but only about 1 in 500 causes damage. About 100 of these are level 6 quakes, 20 are level 7 quakes and 1 or 2, level 8 quakes.

GET THIS!

If records are to be believed the worst earthquake of all happened in Syria and northern Egypt during the Crusades in 1201. Over 1 million people were killed.

Mr Richter

The strength of an earthquake is measured on a scale invented by Charles Richter in 1935 and called the Richter Scale. It goes from 0 to 9, and each level is 10 times stronger than the previous level. Level 9 is over 40,000 times more powerful than the atomic bomb dropped on Hiroshima.

Big shakes

The most powerful earthquake was in Japan in 1933. It reached level 8.9 and killed 2,990 people. Only 10 years before, a level 8.3 quake in Japan killed 143,000 people.

British shakes

Believe it or not there are even earthquakes in Britain. The biggest known happened in 1931 on the Dogger Bank in the North Sea. It reached level 6. Bet that shook the fish up a lot!

Hot water

Geysers are like giant pressure cookers – superheated steam and water are thrown out of the ground in explosive jets. The highest natural geyser in the world is the Steamboat Geyser in the Yellowstone National Park in Wyoming, USA. It ejects water to a height of 115m.

Awesome oceans

Of the four major oceans – the Pacific, the Atlantic, the Indian and the Arctic – the Pacific is the biggest. It covers over 179.6 million sq km. That's more than all the land on the Earth's surface.

The oceans contain about 1,377 quintillion litres of water. If that were shared out among every person on Earth we would each have 8.2 million litres for every day of our life. That's enough for over 105,000 baths every day!

── GET THIS! ──
The sea contains traces of gold. There are 4g in every billion kg of seawater, or over 5 billion kg of gold in total. It's so diluted it's not worth the huge cost of extraction.

Luscious lakes

It's all very well having all that sea water, but we can't drink it. We need fresh water. Only 2.6% of all the world's water is fresh.

The world's wettest lakes

Lake Baikal in Russia wins the prize for the deepest lake – it's over 1.6km deep.
Let's take a look at the 10 biggest freshwater lakes in the world.

Very salty

Not all lakes are fresh water. The Caspian Sea is really a lake because it's entirely surrounded by land. It's nearly 12 times the size of Lake Baikal. But it's full of salt water.

── GET THIS! ──
The Dead Sea, on the border of Israel and Jordan, is so full of salt that it is 16% more dense than fresh water, making it impossible for anyone to sink in it. So you don't need armbands when you're learning to swim.

Raging rivers

Rivers account for only 0.028% of all the fresh water on the planet, but this still amounts to about 10.5 quadrillion litres.

The longest river in the world is the Nile, at 6,670km. There's another river flowing deep underground below the Nile and it holds 6 times more water than the Nile.

Amazing Amazon

The Amazon holds the most water. On average the river contains about 1,360 trillion litres.

Incredibly, if the second and third longest rivers, the Amazon and the Yangtze-Kiang, were placed end to end, they would reach almost exactly from the North Pole to the South Pole through the centre of the Earth.

Rivers are at their most dangerous when they flood. Yet farmers in Egypt rely on the Nile flooding every year to bring water and nutrients to their fields. Without these floods there would have been no Egyptian civilization and no Pyramids.

The most dangerous river for flooding is the Hwang-He or Yellow River, known as China's Sorrow. The worst ever flood happened in 1931 when over 3,700,000 people died.

Aaaaah!

There are at least five rivers in the world with the name Aa. Pretty obvious name for a river if you stumble across it in the dark.

Lake	Surface area (*square km*)	Volume (trillion gallons)	% of World's lakes & rivers
Baikal	31,494	5,069	14.1%
Tanganyika	32,900	4,021	11.2%
Superior	82,100	2,674	7.5%
Malawi/Nyasa	28,879	1,348	3.8%
Michigan	57,800	1,080	3.0%
Huron	59,600	777	2.2%
Victoria	68,800	553	1.5%
Great Bear	31,330	496	1.4%
Great Slave	28,570	389	1.1%
Ontario	18,960	360	1.0%

The big splash

The highest waterfall in the world is the Angel Falls in south-east Venezuela, but it's really no more than a runny nose! What water there is plummets down 978m. That's $3\frac{1}{4}$ times the height of the Eiffel Tower in Paris.

The most spectacular waterfalls are the Boyoma (or Stanley) Falls in the Democratic Republic of the Congo, Africa. Over 16.8 million litres of water flow over those falls every second.

The Guairá Falls between Brazil and Paraguay used to beat the Boyoma hands down, with over 50 million litres of water flowing over them every second. However, with the building of the Itaipú Dam in 1982, the Falls vanished under the waters.

If the Boyoma Falls get the gold, the silver goes to the Khône Falls in Laos, the widest falls in the world. The Niagara-Horseshoe Falls of Canada only pick up the bronze, with a measly 5.5 million litres per second flowing over them.

Great atmosphere

The Earth's atmosphere extends up to about 900km, but the bit that we breathe and affects us with its weather is very small. It's called the troposphere. This rises to about 15km at the equator but only 8km at the poles.

The temperature of the troposphere falls by about 5°C for every 1,000 metres you rise above sea level.

The average daytime surface temperature of the Earth is about 15°C

the top of Mount Everest is about −30°C

the top of the troposphere is about −55°C.

GET THIS!

Every year mankind chucks over a trillion kg of pollutants into the atmosphere. That's over 3 times the weight of everyone on Earth.

Soggy statistics

There are about 483 billion kg of water vapour in the atmosphere. If it all fell as rain in one go it would cover the United States to a depth of 7.5m.

A single storm cloud may weigh as much as 500 million kg, so never underestimate a rainy day!

GET THIS!

The rainiest day ever recorded was 16 March 1952, when 1.8m fell on Réunion Island in the Indian Ocean.

Take a raincoat when you go to Mount Wai'ale'ale on Kauai in Hawaii. It rains there for 350–60 days every year, more than anywhere else on Earth.

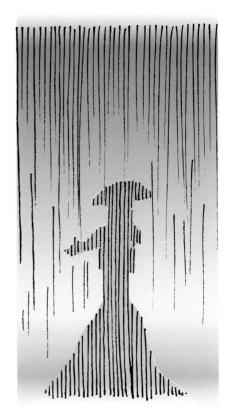

	Place (year)	**Temperature**
Hottest ever	Al' Azizyah, Libya (1922)	57.7°C
Hottest all-year average	Dallol, Ethiopia	34°C
Coldest ever	Vostock, Antarctica (1983)	−89.2°C
Coldest all-year average	Plateau Station, Antarctica	−57°C
Coldest village	Oymyakon, Siberia	−72°C

Lightning strikes

As you're reading this there are about 2,000 thunderstorms occurring all over the Earth. There are over 8 million lightning strikes every day.

How far?

If you count the number of seconds after seeing lightning, until you hear the thunder, then for every 2 seconds the storm is about 1 km away.

Lightning strikes can reach awesome speeds of 50,000–140,000km per second – *that's almost half the speed of light!*

Between 1942 and 1977 Roy Sullivan, a park ranger in Virginia, USA, was struck by lightning 7 times yet survived.

Windy worries

Have you ever felt the wind blow so strongly you thought you'd be blown away? The strongest winds occur in tornadoes – the fastest yet recorded was 450km/h at Wichita Falls in Texas in 1958.

The windiest place in the world is in the Antarctic where there are gales raging at over 175km/h for many months of the year. At least it's not as windy as it is on Neptune.

GET THIS!

A few years ago a lorry driver stopped in Oymyakon in Siberia and, not realizing how cold it was, got out of his cab – within seconds he had frozen to the spot.

The Earth is gradually warming up. This steady increase is believed to be due to the 'greenhouse effect' – where heat is trapped inside the atmosphere owing to a build-up of carbon dioxide.

Freezing facts

A single snowflake weighs as little as one-thousandth of a gram, and yet the total amount of fresh snow that falls each year in the whole world weighs 450 trillion kg. That's trillions of snowflakes and yet it's believed that no two snowflakes ever look the same.

The largest snowflakes that have ever fallen were 38cm across and 20cm thick. They fell at Fort Keogh, Montana on 28 January 1887.

A single snow cloud can drop up to 41 billion kg of snow.

The most snow to fall on 1 day was 1.9m at Silver Lake, Colorado, in April 1921.

More snow falls on Canada than on any other country in the world – an ideal place to hold a snowman building competition?

Avalanche!

Snow can be dangerous stuff. On average about 600,000 tonnes of snow fall in one avalanche, but in 1962 over 2.6 million tonnes of snow fell in an avalanche in Peru.

Frozen solid

80% of the world's fresh water is frozen as ice, snow or permafrost.

Do you want to know what the smelliest thing in the world is, or how hot it can get, or how cold, or the fastest you can go, or the most dangerous thing in the world??? Well, you've come to the right place.

Science is all about why things are the way they are. You'll find lots of other scientific things in this book, stuff about outer space, the Earth, your body, dinosaurs . . .

Here we'll look at the rest of science. From stinky test tubes to incredible powers.

We've got a lot to thank science for. After all you wouldn't have your television or stereo or computer or video games or bike without science.

LAR

SPECTACU

SCIENCE

1.000.000.000.000.000.000.000
000.000.000.000.000.000

We're going to find out about
- the smelliest smells
- the most powerful forces
- the biggest numbers
- the tiniest bits
- the fastest speeds
- the weirdest inventions
... and some nutty professors!

Fastest speed ever

Light is the fastest thing in the Universe. The speed of light is 300,000km per second. To travel all the way round the Earth and back to you it would take just $\frac{1}{8}$ of a second.

Sound travels at 331m per second – a round-the-world trip would take nearly 34 hours!

See it first

Light is over 900,000 times faster than sound. That's why you see lightning before you hear the thunder.

Sound travels 5 times faster under water and 15 times faster through glass!

— GET THIS! —

Scientists have managed to slow light down at super-cool temperatures. They've slowed it down to an amazing 60km/h – you could overtake it on a skateboard!

Supersonic

A rifle bullet can reach 3,623km/h or 3 times the speed of sound. Victims are shot by a bullet before they hear it being fired.

LATER

I'M YOUR GREAT GREAT GREAT GREAT GREAT GREAT GRAMPS.

Warped speed

Strange things happen if you try and travel near the speed of light. If anyone could see you, they'd see you shrinking. You'd also be getting heavier and heavier. Time would slow down so, if you went on a journey at near light-speed, by the time you got back you'd be only a little older, but everyone else would have died centuries ago.

Atomic

There are something like 10^{85} atoms in the Universe. That's

10,000,000,000,000,000,000,000,000,000,
000,000,000,000,000,000,000,000,000,000,
000,000,000,000,000,000

or ten sextillion vigintillion!

93% of all those atoms are hydrogen atoms.

Atoms are tiny. 1 quintillion of them scrunched together would just about cover a pin-head.

The atoms of caesium are the largest of all atoms. If you laid 2 million of them side by side they'd measure 1mm.

Inside the atom are lots of sub-atomic particles. At the centre are a neutron and a proton and whizzing around this nucleus are electrons.

Protons and neutrons are about 1,836 times larger than electrons.

Protons exist for a very, very long time. It has been estimated that the life of a proton is at least 100 decillion (10^{32}) years, or

100,000,000,000,000,000,000,000,
000,000,000 years, which is older than the Universe.

Mega-vision

The most powerful microscope is the atomic force microscope which can magnify a million times, enough to see individual atoms.

The Hubble Space Telescope, in orbit round the Earth, is the best optical telescope of all. It can see almost to the edge of the Universe and so back to the beginning of time!

Happy landing

If you fall out of a plane, the fastest you'll plummet to Earth is about 180km/h – the air stops you falling any faster. Unfortunately, you'd be unlikely to survive.

The furthest anyone has fallen without a parachute and survived is 6,700m. Lieutenant Chisov of the Russian Air Force struck the ground on the edge of a snow-covered ravine and slid the rest of the way. Please don't try this at home.

─── GET THIS! ───

The most amazing survival was by Flight Sergeant Nicholas Alkemade in 1944. His Lancaster bomber was on fire and his parachute had burned. He jumped out and fell 5,486m in little over a minute, landed in a fir tree and was thrown into a deep snow bank which broke his fall. He didn't break a single bone!

Now you see it . . . now you don't

There are 92 elements that occur naturally on Earth. All the others are created artificially.

Seaborgium is so artificial and hates being created so much that it disappears in less than 30 seconds.

Elementary

Aluminium is the commonest metal on Earth yet was not discovered until 1825.

Only 2 elements are liquids at normal temperatures. Yet one of them, mercury, is a metal. The other one stinks so much it is called 'bromine' from the Greek bromos meaning 'stench'.

Gallium is a metal that is used in computers to make them work faster. However, gallium melts if you hold it in your hand. If you squeeze it, it turns to liquid, like ice to water.

HIYA HUBBLE

Super-pong

There are 17,000 known distinct smells in the world, and you can produce several of them, some of them very smelly indeed. However, your nose can probably only identify 5,000.

The worst smell in the world is ethyl mercaptan. It's even worse than all your dad's old socks scrunched together. It's the smell produced by skunks. You'd be able to smell it even if there was less than a teaspoonful of it hidden somewhere in your school playground.

Icy cold

The coldest it can ever get is absolute zero. That's –273.15°C.

That's colder than the surface of Pluto, the coldest planet in the solar system. It has a surface temperature of –230°C.

The coldest liquid you can get is liquid helium. Helium turns into a liquid at –268°C which is pretty close to absolute zero.

Liquid helium is weird stuff as it flows uphill!

If you dropped a banana into liquid helium you could shatter it with a hammer.

GET THIS!

The great white shark can smell a single drop of blood in 4.6 million litres of water.

GET THIS!

It should be impossible to reach absolute zero because at that point all motion ceases, including the movement of sub-atomic particles. However, in 1993 the Low Temperature Laboratory in Helsinki achieved a temperature only 0.28 billionths of a degree above absolute zero. This is colder than the coldest depths of space.

As water freezes it expands – it's the only substance to do this. Other things contract when they get colder. Water expands into ice with a force equal to 140kg per sq cm – enough to squash you flat. That's why frozen water pipes burst.

Whoops

Methane is one of the gases we all produce when we break wind.

It has been estimated that the sheep in New Zealand produce enough methane to meet the entire fuel needs of the country.

A small flock of sheep produces enough methane to power a family car.

Hot, hot, hot

The temperature of your body is about 36.9°C (unless you're ill with flu when it gets a bit higher).

The hottest place on Earth reaches 57.7°C – pretty uncomfortable, but nothing compared with how hot it gets on Venus: 460°C!

The centre of the Sun reaches an incredible 15 million °C but we've actually managed to create a temperature far hotter than that: 510 million °C.

Biggest numbers

A googol is such a huge number it's enough to make you go googol-eyed.

It's 10 to the power of 100 (10^{100}) or

10,000,000,000,000,000,000,000, 000,000,000,000,000,000,000,000, 000,000,000,000,000,000,000,000, 000,000,000,000,000,000,000,000, 000,000.

The figure is so big that the chap who suggested it, Edward Kasner, believes that that many words have yet to be spoken by everyone who ever lived since the dawn of time.

Mind boggling

Kasner created an even bigger number called the googolplex. This is a googol to the power of a googol and is such a big number that there isn't enough space in the known Universe to write it out in full.

The googolplex is so big that from the time the Universe began to the time when all matter decays and the Universe is no more, we will not be even a millionth of the way towards a googolplex number of seconds.

Big numbers are difficult to picture. They have names that end in -illion, but can also be expressed as multiples of the number 10. So 1 million is 10 x 10 x 10 x 10 x 10 x 10, which is 10 multiplied by itself 6 times. This is usually shown as 10^6, the 6 showing how many times the number is multiplied by itself. It also shows how many noughts the number has.

Million	10^6	1,000,000
Billion	10^9	1,000,000,000
Trillion	10^{12}	1,000,000,000,000
Quadrillion	10^{15}	1,000,000,000,000,000
Quintillion	10^{18}	1,000,000,000,000,000,000
Sextillion	10^{21}	1,000,000,000,000,000,000,000
Septillion	10^{24}	1,000,000,000,000,000,000,000,000
Octillion	10^{27}	1,000,000,000,000,000,000,000,000,000
Nonillion	10^{30}	1,000,000,000,000,000,000,000,000,000,000
Decillion	10^{33}	1,000,000,000,000,000,000,000,000,000,000,000
Vigintillion	10^{63}	1,000,000,000,000,000,000,000,000,000,000,000,000,000, 000,000,000,000,000,000,000,000,000
Trigintillion	10^{93}	1,000,000,000,000,000,000,000,000,000,000,000,000,000, 000,000,000,000,000,000,000,000,000,000,000,000,000,000, 000,000,000,000

No space for tears

In space astronauts can't cry properly because there is no gravity and tears won't flow. It's quite a job going to the toilet as well!

GET THIS!

The very first electronic computer, made in 1946, weighed 30 tonnes, covered 1,400 sq m, and had 800km of wire. It could do 5,000 calculations a second. The most powerful modern computer can do nearly 2 trillion operations per second.

Learn by our mistakes!

It pays to be untidy. In 1928 Alexander Fleming left some old culture pots full of germs lying about in his laboratory. Some bits of mould fell into these pots and a few days later Fleming discovered the mould had killed off the bacteria. When he examined the mould more carefully he was able to isolate penicillin.

In 1919 Harry Pickup was cleaning out an old ammunitions factory when he dropped some explosive down the toilet. He discovered it did wonders to the dirty toilet, so he went into the toilet-cleaning business!

The maddest scientist

Al-Hasen, who lived nearly 1,000 years ago, was a clever but boastful man. He claimed he could control the flooding of the Nile. The Caliph heard of this and hired Al-Hasen to do the job. But Al-Hasen didn't know how to do it, and didn't dare admit this because the Caliph was famous for his cruelty. So Al-Hasen had to pretend to be mad, and keep up the pretence until the Caliph died many years later.

In 1845 the Swiss chemist Christian Schönbein was experimenting in his kitchen at home. His wife had told him not to do this, but she was out. Unfortunately Schönbein spilt some nitric acid and sulphuric acid on the floor. In a panic he wiped it up with the nearest thing to hand – his wife's apron. He then hung the apron over the stove to dry. However, when the apron dried it exploded. Schönbein had discovered nitrocellulose – a powerful explosive.

Man's greatest achievement

Injections may not be much fun, but they save a lot of lives. Smallpox was a deadly disease and killed 1 in 4 of those who caught it (and many people did). In 1796 Edward Jenner successfully inoculated a boy against smallpox. In 1967 the World Health Organization began a global campaign of inoculation and by 1980 smallpox had been eradicated – the first time any disease had been destroyed.

GET THIS!

The most powerful acid is fluoro-antimonic acid. It's 20 quintillion times stronger than concentrated sulphuric acid.

Whose idea was that?

People invent the strangest things.

Lighter-than-air furniture. Furniture filled with lighter-than-air gases so that when not in use it floats up to the ceiling.

The Whisper Seat. A toilet seat with a special lining so that you can't hear people going to the toilet.

Chewing-gum locket. A container for used chewing gum, to keep it safe in case you want to chew it again.

Chicken glasses. To protect the chicken's eyes from being pecked.

Parrot nappy. A tiny nappy to stop parrots from dirtying the furniture.

Things not worth inventing:

- waterproof toilet paper
- cat flap for the fridge
- night-time sundial
- fireproof matches
- toenail glue
- barcode for zebras
- insoluble sugar
- unsinkable anchor
- chocolate saucepan
- indelible soap

Bitter end

Scientific research can get a bit dangerous at times.

In 1626 Francis Bacon had the cool idea that snow might preserve things – like modern fridges do. He leapt out of his carriage on Hampstead Heath, bought a chicken and started stuffing it with snow. (The chicken was dead by the way.) Bacon caught a chill that went to his chest, and he died.

In AD 79 Pliny wanted to study the eruption of the volcano Vesuvius at close hand. He got a bit too close, was overcome by the fumes and died.

The Swedish chemist Karl Scheele probably created more new chemical compounds than anyone else. He also had the dangerous habit of tasting them. Amazingly he tasted the highly poisonous hydrogen cyanide and lived. But he also tasted various compounds of mercury, and they got him. He died of mercury poisoning.

MYSTERIOUS

X-FILES

The world is a mysterious place and there are things going on we don't really understand. Have you ever heard things crawling about in your bedroom at night – and there's nothing there!!!???

Have you lost things even though they were there just seconds before? Or seen things you couldn't believe existed – like a clean pair of socks or a $50 note!!!

Have you seen odd shapes in the sky, and they aren't next-door's washing? Or seen strange lights, or ghosts or monsters? Or have you ever dreamed something that later seemed to come true???

I'd better stop before I summon up dark forces. This section looks at lots of those incredible myths, magics and mysteries that we can't explain.

The most incompetent ghost?

A house in Thetford, Norfolk, was reputedly haunted by a one-legged Jesuit priest. In 1974 police were called to the house when a burglar alarm went off. They were amazed to see a single row of footprints across a room ending at a brick wall. It seems the ghost had vanished through the wall but then set off the burglar alarm!

Spookiest spots

The title 'the most haunted house in England' was long held by Borley Rectory in Suffolk. For over 60 years there were claims of phantom footsteps and of the ghost of a nun floating around the grounds. The remains of a woman were found in the Rectory in 1943, but no one knows if she was the ghostly nun.

GET THIS!

The first reference to a haunted house goes back over 4,000 years to the time of the Sumerians.

The most haunted village in Britain is allegedly Pluckley in Kent. There are at least 13 different ghosts there including one of the local schoolmaster who hanged himself from a tree. There is also a farm with phantom smells, and a house with phantom whispers!

GET THIS!

Every year on the anniversary of the Battle of Edgehill (23 October) the ghosts of the soldiers are allegedly seen refighting the battle. Imagine if that happened with football matches!

Second time around?

Many people have recalled past lives under hypnosis. One person recalled being the mother of a family of children in Ireland in the early 1900s. She traced the children, who had since grown up, and could remember details of their lives even though she had never met them before.

Space goblins?

Perhaps the weirdest of all stories about aliens happened in 1955 at a farm in Kentucky. The people living at the farm had to shut themselves in when they were menaced by several small, 'glowing', goblin-like creatures with large saucer-like eyes and arms twice as long as their legs. Bullets fired at these creatures had no effect. It was several hours before the family could escape. Was it a prank, did they make it up, or did it really happen?

Ape-men

Are you abominable? Do you have big feet? Maybe you're a Yeti or Sasquatch. These strange ape-like creatures have never been captured but are believed to live in Tibet and remote parts of North America. Some people believe they may be surviving examples of distant human ancestors.

Nessie the slug

The weirdest sighting of the Loch Ness monster was not in the loch but on land. In 1933 Mr and Mrs Spicer saw this globby grey thing wobbling over a road by the side of the loch. They described it as 'a huge snail with a long neck'.

Vanished!

I bet there are some people you'd like to see vanish off the face of the Earth. It does happen.

All aboard! The most famous disappearance of all time is that of the crew and passengers of the ship the *Mary Celeste.* This ship was found abandoned in the mid-Atlantic in 1872. There was no one on board, and it looked like the boat had been abandoned suddenly. Although many ideas have been put forward, from abduction by aliens to madness and mutiny, no one knows what happened.

Flushed away. In 1968 Jerrold Potter went into the toilet on a plane while on a flight to Dallas, Illinois. The plane shuddered slightly, Jerrold was never seen again.

Hot air? In 1881 the MP Walter Powell was carried away in a balloon and never seen again. No debris was ever found of the balloon, the basket or him.

Lost army. In 1915, during the dreadful Gallipoli campaign of World War I, a troop of some 260 men of the Norfolk regiment marched into a wood and disappeared without trace.

Kaspar the wonder boy

In 1828 a 17-year-old urchin turned up at Nuremberg and started an amazing mystery. He could hardly talk but had letters that said he had been kept all his life alone in a dungeon with a boarded-up window. He could see in the dark and had uncanny powers of smell and hearing. He said his name was Kaspar Hauser. Mysteriously, he was murdered. No one ever found out who he was or where he came from.

The man in the iron mask

From 1669 to 1703 a man was kept imprisoned in France and all that time wore an iron mask. Who was he? Many thought he was the elder brother of the king, Louis XIV, and so the real heir to the throne. It's more likely that Louis XIV was himself illegitimate, and the prisoner a half-brother whom Louis resembled. If this was discovered, Louis would be deposed. Not wanting his brother killed, Louis instead had him imprisoned and his face hidden so no one could see the family resemblance.

GET THIS!

The Dutch psychic, Gerard Croiset, could trace missing people by visions he had when he touched their clothing or possessions. He helped the police track down many missing children. What visions would your old clothes produce!?

Just a coincidence?

When Anne Parrish was in a second-hand book shop in Paris in the 1920s she saw a book of fairy tales she used to love as a child in the United States. When she opened the book she found her name and address inside. It was the very copy she had had as a child.

Two Umberto's

In 1900 King Umberto I of Italy visited a restaurant in Monza and was surprised at how alike he and the restaurant owner were – another Umberto. They discovered they had been born and had married on the same day, and that the names of their wives and their sons were the same. The next day the king learned to his horror that his double had been killed in a shooting accident. As he discussed the tragedy, King Umberto was assassinated.

In 1889 a man was killed in his back garden when he was struck by lightning. About 30 years later his son was killed by lightning in exactly the same spot, and 20 years after that, the grandson as well.

Bermuda moped

In July 1974 Neville Ebbin was killed when he was knocked off his moped by a taxi in Bermuda. Exactly a year later, his brother Erskine was killed in the same place when he was knocked off the same moped by the same taxi, with the same driver and the same passenger!

Double trouble

There are loads of coincidences involving twins. Here are just a couple.

Twins born in 1939 were adopted by different families and knew nothing of each other. Yet both were christened James, both had a brother called Larry and a dog called Toy. Both married women called Linda. Both divorced and remarried women called Betty. Both had sons called James. Both worked as petrol pump attendants. Both liked stock-car racing. And both had holidays each year in the same hotel in Florida!

Dorothy Collins lived in Sussex while her twin sister Marjorie lived in South Africa, but both died at the same moment in April 1961.

Miraculous moments

The Indian mystic Sai Baba performs in front of thousands of people, materializing food, flowers and ashes. He lifts himself and others into the air, appears in two places at once and reputedly even raises the dead. No one knows how he does it.

The healing power of the water at Lourdes in France is legendary. Jack Traynor was paralysed in one arm, suffered from epilepsy and could not walk. In 1923 he bathed in the waters at Lourdes and within 4 days was fit and healthy.

BBZZZZZZZZ!

Buzz off

Bees have been known to attend the funerals of their beekeepers. At the funeral of Sam Rogers in 1934 thousands of his bees swarmed to the cemetery and settled about his coffin.

Flaming nuisance

Do your feet sometimes get so hot you think your socks are going to explode? Well that's nothing. Some people suddenly burst into flames. It's called spontaneous combustion. In 1922 Euphemia Johnson was sitting drinking a cup of tea when she burst into flames. Her body ended up as a pile of ashes, but her clothes and the chair she was sitting on were not burned!

Hover craft

Daniel Dunglas Home was a famous Victorian psychic. He may have been just a clever magician, but one of his 'tricks' has never been explained. In 1868 Home floated out of one window on the third floor and then floated back in another window in the next room! Don't try it – you're more likely to plummet than float!

What happens next?

Wouldn't it be handy to be able to see into the future? Get a look at those exam questions in advance? Or would you find out something you really didn't want to know?

- In 1812 Countess Toutschkoff dreamed that her father told her her husband would die at Borodino. She warned her husband but neither of them had ever heard of Borodino. A few months later the Count was killed at the Battle of Borodino.

- The wife of Ulysses S. Grant had a terrible foreboding on the morning of 14 April 1865 and persuaded her husband not to go to the theatre that night. That was the night Abraham Lincoln was assassinated. Apparently Grant was also on the assassin's 'hit list'.

- In 1912 as Mrs Marshall watched a liner steam out of Southampton she suddenly shouted, 'That ship is going to sink !' The ship was the *Titanic*, which struck an iceberg and sank 4 days later.

- The night before Exeter in Devon suffered a bombing raid in 1942, hundreds of cats were seen leaving the city as if they knew something terrible was about to happen.

Predictability

Many people have claimed they can see into the future. One of the most impressive was Jeane Dixon. In 1956 she foresaw the assassination of President John F. Kennedy which happened in 1963. She also had a sudden vision of the death of actress Carole Lombard after they shook hands. She warned the actress not to fly but a few days later she was killed in an air crash.

GET THIS!

Did dinosaurs have guns or have people travelled through time? Some claim that fossils of a few prehistoric animals have been found with bullet holes in them!

Did they really exist?

Mermaids
Top half human, bottom half fish. Sightings continue to be reported. Maybe just wishful thinking by sailors long at sea.

Centaurs
Legs and body of a horse, top half human. It's possible that when humans first learned to ride horses, some early, not-very-bright witnesses believed that horse and rider were one creature.

Griffins
Head and wings of an eagle, body of a lion. More likely to be the bearded vulture, a large bird with a mane of feathers. They are capable of carrying away lambs and dogs.

Dragons
Large flying reptiles. Large reptiles, like the Komodo dragon, do exist but none flies. Pterodactyls and other flying dinosaurs were extinct long before humans appeared. No more recent remains of large flying reptiles have been found.

Unicorn
A horse with a single horn. Although this may well have sprung from early sightings of a rhinoceros, this does not account for the legendary grace of the unicorn. It may be that it became confused with the okapi, which looks more like a horse. Sailors may also have brought back the horn of the narwhal to spin their own legend.

WHAT DID THEY REALLY DO FOR US?

Do you know what your grandfather did, or your great-grandfather? Do you know how many ancestors you've got? Just consider – your father's father's father . . . and so on about 90 times . . . was alive at the time of Julius Caesar. If you go back another 90 times your ancestors were around when Stonehenge was being built. There's a little bit of them in you – and they're part of history.

So is history boring? Some of it is – yawn – but some of it is odd, amazing, amusing and incredible. History goes back about 12,000 years to the start of civilization – before that, it's *pre*history (see page 32–41).

During that time

- over 100 billion people have lived or are still living
- there have been about 500 generations
- there have been about 16,000 kings and queens
- there have been countless wars and battles
- humans have landed on the Moon
- just about every stupid thing you can do has been done!

In this section you'll find

- the oldest, youngest and smelliest rulers
- the maddest and most dangerous rulers
- the first things invented and by whom
- the brightest and the barmiest people
- the last things some people said

. . . and a lot more.

First country

The very first country ever was Sumeria, in what is now Iraq. It was here that the biblical Garden of Eden was believed to exist and where the first kings anywhere in the world began to rule back in about 3800 BC.

Ancient walls

Jericho is the oldest regularly occupied city in the world. People have lived there for nearly 9,000 years. They have built some new houses since then, though.

For my first trick

The Sumerians and their successors, the Babylonians, were a bright lot, and invented most of the basics of civilization. The Sumerians invented writing, wheeled transport, maps and soap. The Babylonians added the clock and written numbers (so maths is all their fault). And that was all before 2000 BC. They didn't get round to everything, though. It was down to the Moguls of India to invent ice cream, which they did in about AD 1500.

Great Greeks

The Greeks must have had more than their fair share of brain cells too.

- In 585 BC Thales of Miletus was the first to predict an eclipse of the Sun. It happened exactly when he said it would. The eclipse so frightened the Medes and the Lydians, who were fighting each other at the time, that they stopped their battle and made peace. This is the earliest event we can date precisely, 28 May 585 BC.

- Empedocles came up with the theory of evolution 2,200 years before Darwin. Empedocles was so full of his own importance that he believed he could jump into the volcano of Mount Etna and be raised up to heaven as a god. That was the end of him!

- In about 270 BC Aristarchus (not Harry Starkers) worked out that the Moon was $\frac{1}{3}$ the size of the Earth and that the Earth revolved around the Sun.

- In 240 BC, Eratosthenes worked out the circumference of the Earth using only a stick and got it right to within a few hundred kilometres. No one could prove his figure until del Cano sailed round the world 1,800 years later. How do you think he did it?*

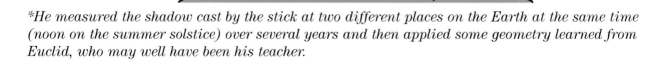

He measured the shadow cast by the stick at two different places on the Earth at the same time (noon on the summer solstice) over several years and then applied some geometry learned from Euclid, who may well have been his teacher.

Bold, brave and barmy

Greek and Roman history is full of tales of brave heroes. They may be a tad exaggerated of course.

- In 510 BC Horatius held back the entire Etruscan army single-handedly while his fellow Romans cut down the bridge across the Tiber to stall the invasion.

- In 490 BC an army of 10,000 Greeks defeated 100,000 Persians at the Battle of Marathon.

- In 480 BC, Leonidas of Sparta defended the pass at Thermopylae with only 300 men against nearly 200,000 Persians. Needless to say the Persians won, but not before 20,000 had been killed!

Savage Caesars

Lots of Roman emperors were both brutal and bonkers.

- Because Caligula was going bald he made it a crime punishable by death to look down on his head. He loved horses and brought his favourite horse, Incitatus, to senate meetings and suggested making him consul.

- Nero fancied himself as a whizz on the lyre. He forced people to listen to his musical recitals which were, apparently, pretty dreadful. If they didn't listen he had them put to death.

- In AD 215 Caracalla ordered that thousands of the young men of Alexandria be rounded up and slaughtered because one of them upset him.

GET THIS!

Around 230 BC Archimedes claimed "Give me a place to stand and a lever long enough and I could move the world". When challenged he set up a series of levers and pulleys and single-handedly lifted a fully laden ship out of the harbour.

Ancient wonders

In about 150 BC a Greek engineer named Philon thought it would be a whizz idea to come up with the Seven Wonders of the World – not the most amazing footballers of the day, but the greatest buildings and works of art. Here's his list.

Wonder	When built	When destroyed
Pyramids at Giza (Egypt)	*c.* 2550 BC	still there
Hanging Gardens of Babylon	*c.* 600 BC	482 BC
Statue of Zeus at Olympia	432 BC	462
Mausoleum at Halicarnassus	362–344 BC	1522
Temple of Artemis at Ephesus	*c.* 330–290 BC	262
Colossus of Rhodes	302–290 BC	227 BC
Pharos of Alexandria	299–280 BC	1375

The Colossus of Rhodes (a giant statue of the sun god Helios about 32m high) is one of the best known of the Seven Wonders though it stood for only 63 years before it was destroyed by an earthquake.

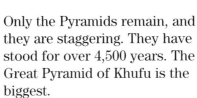

Only the Pyramids remain, and they are staggering. They have stood for over 4,500 years. The Great Pyramid of Khufu is the biggest.

- It's 147m high
- It covers 49,726 sq m
- It took 2.3 million blocks of stone to build
- It weighs 5,216,400 tonnes.

── GET THIS! ──

All 3 pyramids at Giza contain enough stone to build a wall 3m high and 0.3m wide all the way round France.

You could fit both the Houses of Parliament and St Paul's Cathedral into the Great Pyramid and still have room to spare.

The Pharos was a lighthouse, and was the second highest building in the world at the time, after the Pyramids. It was probably 140m high and was the world's first skyscraper. No other European building was higher until Old St Paul's Cathedral and Lincoln Cathedral were built 1,600 years later.

And more . . .

The Seven Wonders weren't the only incredible buildings in the Ancient World – they just happened to be the ones Philon knew about. Here are some other incredible ancient wonders.

Stonehenge, England

The most famous stone circle in the world. It's about 4,000 years old. There are over 30 huge upright stones with stones laid over the top. The biggest weighs 50 tonnes and is 9m long. There are 80 smaller stones, each weighing up to 4 tonnes.

Amazingly, these stones were brought all the way from Wales, over 385km away. And we still don't really know how.

Reach for the sky

Buildings keep getting taller and taller.

The Great Wall of China

This was built over 2,200 years ago by order of the very first Chinese emperor, Shih Huang-ti, who was power mad.

The wall goes on and on for over 6,400km – further than from London to Chicago.

At places it's 14m high and 10m wide. Five horses could ride side by side along the ramparts.

Thousands died building it, and many were buried in the Wall.

It has been said that the Great Wall is the only man-made object on Earth that can be seen from the surface of the Moon without a telescope, but unfortunately this is not true. That would be incredible!

Statues of Easter Island

Easter Island is a tiny remote island in the Pacific Ocean about 3,600km from Chile. When Admiral Jakob Roggeveen discovered it in 1722 he thought the island was protected by giants with big ears. He then realized that these were giant statues – over 600 of them. The biggest are 11m high and weigh 80 tonnes.

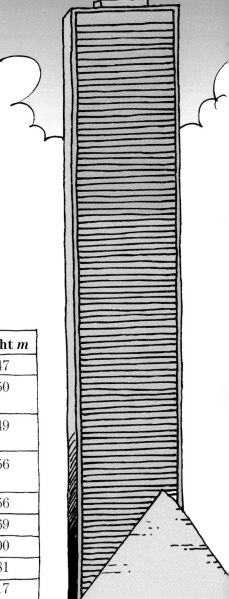

Building	When built	Height *m*
Pyramid of Khufu, Giza, Egypt	2550 BC	147
Lin-He Pagoda, Hangchow, China (destroyed 1121)	970	150
Old St Paul's Cathedral, London, England (spire destroyed 1561)	1315	149
Rouen Cathedral, Rouen, France (destroyed 1822)	1530	156
Cologne Cathedral, Cologne, Germany	1880	156
Washington Memorial, Washington DC, USA	1885	169
Eiffel Tower, Paris, France	1889	300
Empire State Building, New York, USA	1931	381
World Trade Center, New York, USA	1973	417
Sears Tower, Chicago, USA	1974	443
CN Tower, Toronto, Canada	1975	553

Kinquering Congs*

The greatest conqueror of all time was Genghis Khan who from 1206 to 1227 established the Mongol Empire stretching from the Pacific Ocean to the Caspian Sea. He conquered over 12.5 million sq km.

The second greatest conqueror was Alexander the Great. Between 334 and 326 BC he conquered about 5.6 million sq km.

GET THIS!

In 525 BC the Persian king Cambyses defeated the Egyptians by using their religion against them. The Egyptians worshipped the cat so, at the siege of Memphis, the Persians bombarded the city with dead cats. The Egyptians surrendered.

Children in charge

Ever fancied being a king or a queen? Maybe you'd get your own way more.

Mary, Queen of Scots, became queen in 1542, when she was only 7 days old.

Henry VI of England became king in 1422, when he was 8 months 25 days old.

Too heavy

Queen Anne liked to eat a lot. She was so heavy that she couldn't walk and had to be carried to her coronation.

* see about William Spooner on page 88.

20-minute monarch

Crown Prince Luis Filipe of Portugal was mortally wounded on 1 February, 1908, at the same time that his father, King Carlos, was shot dead. Luis, who briefly became Luis III of Portugal, died 20 minutes later.

Regal wrinkly

Pepy II was pharaoh of Egypt for 94 years from 2278–2184 BC, and was 104 when he died. No king has ruled for longer.

King Pong

The title of smelliest ruler in the world is well contended but the winner was probably King Louis XIV of France who apparently had only three baths in his whole lifetime (and he lived for nearly 77 years).

Another whiffmungus contender was King Frederick the Great of Prussia who hardly ever changed his clothes – they'd rot to his back.

Gone with the wind

When the Earl of Oxford bowed to Elizabeth I of England he broke wind. He was so worried about what she might do that he left Britain for 7 years.

Half-inch rulers

Attila the Hun, who ruled over half of Europe in AD 450, was only about 1.2m tall.

Pepin the Short, king of the Franks from AD 751, was 1.37m tall, but he had a big sword – 1.8m long. He also had a huge wife, known as Bertha Bigfoot.

Mad monarchs

Charles VI of France believed his legs and bottom were made of glass and feared travelling in case he shattered.

His grandson, Henry VI of England, had bouts of memory loss and had no idea where his one and only son came from.

George III of Great Britain once reputedly talked to a tree, convinced it was the King of Prussia.

Menelek II of Abyssinia so liked the idea of the electric chair that he ordered 3 – and then discovered there was no electricity in Abyssinia. So he used one of the chairs as his throne.

Ludwig II of Bavaria decided that day was night and night was day. He populated the forests of Bavaria with clockwork bears.

Maniac monarchs

The Mongol warlord Tamerlane known as Timur the lame, had no sense of humour and executed anyone who cracked a joke.

Vlad the Impaler was so called because he would impale his enemies on sharp stakes. He is believed to be the original Count Dracula, and was among the first to use germ warfare. During his war against the Turks in the 1460s, he brought together an army of people suffering from the most disgusting, contagious diseases and sent them into the Turkish camps.

Ivan IV of Russia was known as Ivan the Terrible because he was so bowel-emptyingly vicious. On one occasion he had the entire population of Novgorod, all 50,000, drowned in a freezing river.

For king and country!

The bloodiest battle in the history of the world was the Battle of Stalingrad during World War II, fought between the Germans and the Russians. Around 2 million soldiers were killed.

In World War I over 1 million soldiers were killed in the Battle of the Somme. The noise of the battle could be heard in London.

GET THIS!

More soldiers died during the Crimean War from disease than from fighting.

Dodgy death

In 892, Sigurd the Mighty, earl of Orkney, was bitten to death by the man he'd just killed. Sigurd had cut the head off Maelbrigte of Moray and tied the head to his saddle. As he rode away Maelbrigte's teeth rubbed against Sigurd's leg, the cut turned septic and Sigurd died of blood poisoning.

Legless

Fate struck Sir Arthur Aston a nasty blow when he lost his leg in a battle during the English Civil War. Several years later, fate struck again at the Siege of Drogheda, when his leg was snatched and used to beat him to death.

Died on the throne

Both King George II of Britain and Empress Catherine the Great of Russia died of heart failure while going to the toilet.

The Roman emperor Heliogabalus and the English king Edmund Ironside were both murdered while going to the toilet.

Nutty Norsemen

The Vikings had some great nicknames. Of course there were plain Olaf the Red, Olaf the Black and Olaf the White. Here are some others:

- Ingvald the Tree Hewer, king of Vermland (lived *c*. 700)
- Halfdan the Old and Stingy (lived *c*. 780)
- Ragnar Hairy-Breeches, king of Denmark (died 865)
- Sitric the Squinty (died 927)
- Erik Bloodaxe, king of Norway and York (died 954)
- Thorfinn Skull-splitter, jarl of Orkney (died 977)

What would your Viking name be?

Watch your tongue!

If you think English has always been English then think again. If you were whisked back in time just a few hundred years you'd have difficulty understanding what people were saying.

Our language is made up of words that have come from loads of other languages.

- the word 'cool' comes from the Saxon word, *col*
- 'gob' comes from the Celtic, *gob*, meaning bird's beak
- 'mega' comes from the Greek, *megas*, meaning great
- 'vomit' comes from the Latin word *vomere*, meaning to throw up

Some words have changed their meaning completely. If you called someone 'nice' 500 years ago, you'd mean they were stupid. And if you asked for a pudding you wouldn't get yummy treacle pud, you'd get a sheep's stomach full of greasy meat!

Guess who?

Would you like to be remembered as a deadly disease that makes you sick? Daniel Salmon is. He was an American vet who lived 100 years ago. He identified the food-poisoning bacteria now known as salmonella.

Here are a few more names that have slipped into the language.

Nosey Parker
Matthew Parker (1504–75) was noted for his very long nose and his enquiring nature.

The Real McKoy
'Kid' McCoy (1873–1940) was a champion boxer who called himself 'the Real McCoy' to avoid confusion with another boxer called McCoy. Confusingly, the Real McCoy's real name was Norman Selby.

Spoonerism
William Spooner (1844–1930) often switched sounds around without realizing it. So instead of 'Dear old Queen' he might say 'Queer old Dean'.

The last word

Here are some wonderful last words.

'Die, my dear doctor, that's the last thing I shall do!' Lord Palmerston, 1865.

'Either that wallpaper goes or I do.' Oscar Wilde, 1900.

'I've never felt better.' Douglas Fairbanks, Sr, 1939.

'Go away. I'm all right.' H.G. Wells, 1946.

'I'm looking for a loop-hole.' W.C. Fields, 1946, who was reading a Bible on his death-bed.

Grave words

Even gravestones can be funny.

Here lie the bones of Lazy Fred,
Who wasted precious time in
     bed.
Some plaster fell down on his
     head,
and thanks be praised our
     Freddie's dead.
Tomb of Frederick Twitchell,
Leeds

Here lies Matthew Mud,
Death did him no hurt.
When alive he was Mud,
And now dead he's dirt.
Headstone in Watton, Norfolk

Here lie the bones of Joseph
     Jones,
Who ate while he was able;
But, once o'er fed, he dropped
     down dead,
and fell beneath the table.
Headstone in Wolverhampton

Underneath this sod lies John
     Round
Who was lost at sea and never
     found
Headstone in Watton, Norfolk

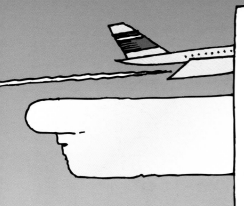

THERE AND BACK AGAIN

How far do you think you travel in a year? Walking, running, skateboarding . . . a couple of hundred kilometres? 1,000? The chances are it's closer to 30,000km and, if you travel much by air, it could be up to 80,000km or more. You probably do a few hundred kilometres a year just to and from school.

A bit different from a few hundred years ago when it would take all day just to travel between towns – unless you had a very fast horse, or it was all down hill in a barrel!

Today you can travel round the world in a few hours, unless of course you try and drive through London first.

But for tens of thousands of years our ancestors travelled everywhere on foot. It's only been 7,000 years since humans domesticated the horse.

In fact, did you know humans could ski before they rode horses? Many would have had toboggans before they had boats!

In this section you'll find out about

- the fastest anyone has travelled
- the furthest anyone's gone
- the biggest and the quickest transport
- who went where first, and how

. . . and who didn't quite make it.

The journey starts here . . .

Made for walking

Did you know that our ancestors first colonized most of the Earth by walking?

By about 15,000 years ago they'd made it to the American continent over a land bridge between what is now Russia and Alaska before sea levels rose.

It took them another 8,000 years to reach the most southerly point of South America. They moved roughly 65km each generation – just far enough to get away from mum and dad!

Snow man

Humans could ski before they could ride! The earliest form of transport was probably the ski – well what would you expect in an Ice Age?

All at sea

Humans didn't put to sea until about 7000 BC. It's believed that the first islands we explored were the Greek islands in the Aegean Sea.

Sea legs

Some scientists think the early humans in Asia might have built boats as early as 800,000 years ago, based on finds made on the island of Flores, in Indonesia. If they didn't build boats they were either excellent swimmers or had remarkably long legs!

Some of the most amazing sea voyages were made by the Polynesians. They sailed across over 3,200km of the Pacific Ocean in dugout canoes locating the smallest of islands.

The wheel was invented around 4000 BC, but the first wheeled vehicle didn't appear until about 1700 BC. The first traffic jams happened a few centuries later.

To boldly go . . .

We don't know about the earliest explorers because no one knew how to write until about 6,000 years ago. You can bet most exploration had been done before anyone wrote about it.

There are only 3 places on Earth where we can be fairly certain who went there first.

Antarctica	John Davis, 7 February 1821. *Davis was an American seal hunter. At the time no one knew he had landed there – he didn't realize it himself. His ship's log-book was not found until 1955.*
South Pole	Roald Amundsen, 14 December 1911. *His expedition beat Robert Scott's by 34 days.*
Deepest part of the ocean	Jacques Piccard and Donald Walsh, 23 January 1960. *They descended 10,916m to the bottom of the Marianas Trench in the Pacific Ocean in a special submarine, or bathyscaphe.*

Myths and myth-takes!

What about all those other famous explorers we've heard about? Well, things aren't always what they seem . . .

Myth 1: Columbus was the first European to reach America.

No he wasn't.

- The Phoenicians almost certainly reached America in about 400 BC.
- It's possible 2 Irish sailors visited America: St Brendan in about AD 550 and Prince Madoc in 1170.
- The Vikings under Leif Eriksson first landed on the northern shores of America in about AD 1000 and settled there for a short while.
- The Norse under Paul Knutson explored the same area in 1356–64.
- In 1398 Henry St Clair, Prince of Orkney, set up Scottish colonies in Labrador and Newfoundland. St Clair was murdered on his return and his colonies were forgotten.

Columbus didn't land on mainland America until 1499. His earlier voyages in 1492–3 took him around the Caribbean islands. John Cabot had already landed in Nova Scotia in 1497.

Myth 2: Magellan was the first to sail round the world.

Tricky – he died about halfway round. Magellan was the first European to cross the Pacific, and prove you *could* sail round the world. However, when he arrived at the Philippines in 1521 he was killed in a war between the islanders. The ships completed their journey back to Spain under the command of Juan Sebastian del Cano.

Myth 3: Robert Peary was the first to reach the North Pole.

Peary claimed to have reached the North Pole on 6 April 1909, but the American Frederick Cook claimed he had already been there on 21 April 1908. Both claims remain unproven. If Peary's and Cook's claims were false, then no one stood at the North Pole until the expedition of the Russian Pavel Geordiyenko in 1948.

Myth 4: Edmund Hillary and Sherpa Tenzing were the first to climb Mount Everest.

Probably, but Everest may already have been climbed. In 1924 George Mallory and Sandy Irvine disappeared during their assault on the summit and were never seen alive again. In 1999 Mallory's body was found sitting in the ice 600m from the top of Everest. Did he make it?

Never seen again

Some intrepid explorers disappeared in mysterious circumstances.

- The Solomon Islands in the Pacific had been discovered in 1567 but their position had been wrongly recorded and no one could find them again. In 1788 Jean de la Pérouse decided to have a go. He set off from Australia and was never seen again. In 1791 Bruni d'Entrecasteaux led an expedition to find Pérouse. He found no trace of him, but he did find the Solomons.

- Ludwig Leichhardt, a short-sighted eccentric, never wore glasses and often had no idea where he was going – not good explorer material! In 1848 he and 6 companions set out to cross Australia from Sydney to Perth. They all disappeared without trace.

- In 1874 Ernest Giles and Alfred Gibson set out to cross Australia. They became lost in a desert. Gibson took their horse and went to find water. Giles followed the horse's tracks on foot. He reached the water hole to find that Gibson had continued on, the horse's tracks heading back into the desert. Giles made it out of the desert, but he never saw Gibson again. The desert is now known as the Gibson Desert.

One step at a time

How far do you walk in a day? That's assuming you get out of bed. If you walk 1 or 2 kilometres a day then you'll only walk about 42,000km in a lifetime.

- Arthur Blessitt walked around the world carrying an 18kg cross. He did the walk over a leisurely 30 years, walked 52,728km and got through 66 pairs of shoes.

- In 1809 Allardyce Barclay was set a challenge to walk 1,000 miles in 1,000 hours. The hours had to follow one after the other but he was allowed to rest provided he walked 1 mile every hour. He kept this up for 42 days and achieved the bet. He became a rich man, because he placed a bet on himself.

Great gallops

In 1676 highwayman William Nevison (known as 'Swift Nick') rode 320km from Rochester, Kent to York in 15 hours – no one knows whether he changed horses. The ride later passed into legend as the ride undertaken by Dick Turpin on his horse Black Bess.

In 1831, for a bet, George Osbaldeston repeated the ride and did it in 8 hours 42 minutes, changing horses 28 times.

Peter Scudamore repeated the journey in 1993 (in almost the same time), and changed horses 48 times.

Voyages of endurance

Sometimes when things get tough, you want to give up. Not these guys.

- Captain William Bligh was turned off his ship following the infamous mutiny on the *Bounty*. In 1789, Bligh and those of his crew who'd remained loyal sailed an open boat 5,826km across the Pacific without a chart, reaching the island of Timor in 47 days.

- In 1895, Joshua Slocum became the first person to sail around the world on his own. It took him 3 years and 70 days to sail 74,000km. Good going for someone who couldn't swim!

- In 1915 Ernest Shackleton and his men lost their ship, the *Endurance*, when it was crushed by the Antarctic ice. They hauled their open boats across ice floes until they reached Elephant Island off the Antarctic coast. Then Shackleton and a few others travelled 1,300km in an open boat to South Georgia Island, walked across the island for 24 hours to seek help, and eventually returned to Elephant Island to rescue the others, who had survived there for 3½ months.

Boats big, wet and wobbly

The biggest ship in the world is the oil tanker *Jahre Viking* – it's 458m long, 69m wide and weighs 573,799 tonnes fully laden. It holds about 650 million litres of oil – enough to fill 300 swimming pools. There's room for 4 full-size football pitches on the deck. Tankers this big need 10km in which to stop and have to allow nearly half an hour to slow down.

One of the strangest ships was the SS *Connector*, built in 1863. It was made in 3 hinged parts so that it undulated over the sea like a caterpillar.

On occasions flat icebergs have been fitted with sails and sailed from the Antarctic to South America.

GET THIS!

The first submarine had to be rowed! It was built in England in 1620 by Cornelius Drebbel. It had a wooden frame covered with leather. It required 12 rowers to make it move, their oars poking out of watertight holes in the side. Drebbel took it for several journeys under the Thames and once took James I with him, who became the first king to travel underwater.

High-speed crossings

The fastest time a boat has ever crossed the Atlantic from the United States to England is 58 hours 35 minutes. It was achieved by the Italian super-yacht *Destriero* in 1992 moving at an average speed of 53 knots (98km/h).

This speed is dwarfed by the official water speed record of 511km/h, achieved by Kenneth Warby in his powerboat *Spirit of Australia* in 1978. That would do the same trans-Atlantic crossing in less than 11.25 hours – though it'd never be able to carry enough fuel.

On yer bike

The bicycle is the most common form of land transport. There are over 800 million in the world, enough to fill every road in Britain 4 times over.

Leonardo da Vinci designed a perfectly good bicycle as early as 1493 but no one got round to building one until Kirkpatrick Macmillan in 1839.

There were bicycles made in the 1790s, but they didn't have any pedals so you had to push them along with your feet.

From 1884 to 1887 Thomas Stevens cycled round the world on a penny-farthing bicycle. He was the first to cycle round the world – well, the dry bits.

The fastest a cyclist has ever ridden on the flat is 105km/h. If you tuck in behind another vehicle (called slipstreaming) you can go much faster. The record is 268.83km/h.

Riding in my car . . .

There are over 500 million cars in the world.

The first petrol-driven car was built by Siegfried Marcus in 1873 but it looked more like a motorized wheelbarrow. He had very little control over it and the police ordered him off the roads.

It was not until the 1890s that cars looking like ones we know today began to appear.

The first traffic lights were introduced in London in 1868 to help control the reckless horse-drawn carriages. However, the flapping signals frightened the horses and only added to the problem. They were gas-powered and one day they blew up.

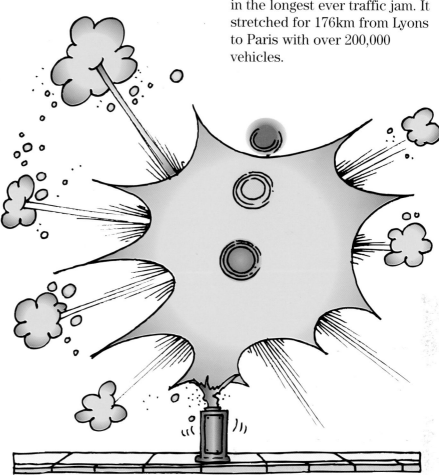

Longest traffic jam

Drivers in France were going nowhere fast on 16 February 1980 because they were stuck in the longest ever traffic jam. It stretched for 176km from Lyons to Paris with over 200,000 vehicles.

Burning rubber

The world's fastest car is the Jaguar XJ220 which has been driven at 349km/h. However, the McLaren F1 6.1 has apparently reached 370km/h in trials. This is also the world's most expensive car, costing over £634,500.

The fastest anyone has ever driven a car is 1,228km/h. This is the world land speed record, set in 1997 by the jet-engine-powered *Thrust SSC*. It was the first car to beat the sound barrier. At that speed you'd get from London to Edinburgh in 33 minutes.

Road works

The first people to build roads in a big way were the Persians. Their great Royal Road was built in about 510 BC. It ran for 2,400km from Sardis to Susa, and took 3 months to walk.

The Romans were *the* great road builders. By the year AD 200 they had completed about 400,000km of road throughout the Roman Empire – more than the total mileage of roads in Britain today – and no cars!

Around 10,000km of road were built in Britain during the first 40 years of Roman occupation.

The longest road in the world today is the Pan-American Highway which runs all the way from Alaska to Chile, a distance of 25,300km. At the UK speed limit of 70mph (112km/h), it would take over 224 hours non-stop to do the journey. *Thrust SSC* would do it in 21 hours.

Keeping track of trains

There are about 1.2 million km of railway track throughout the world. That's enough to go to and from the Moon 3 times.

The longest continuous railway track is the Trans-Siberian railway from Moscow to Nakhodka in Russia. It's 9,438km long, or long enough to go about a quarter of the way round the world.

The fastest trains in the world run in France. The *TGV Atlantique* holds the record at 515km/h. That would complete the Trans-Siberian railway in 18.3 days non-stop.

Up and over

The oldest surviving bridge in the world is at Izmir in Turkey and was built in about 850 BC.

The longest bridge in the world is the causeway across Lake Pontchartrain in Louisiana, USA. It's 38.4km long.

GET THIS!

There are about 25 million km of roads in the world. This length of road would stretch to and from the Moon nearly 66 times. A quarter of all those roads are in the United States.

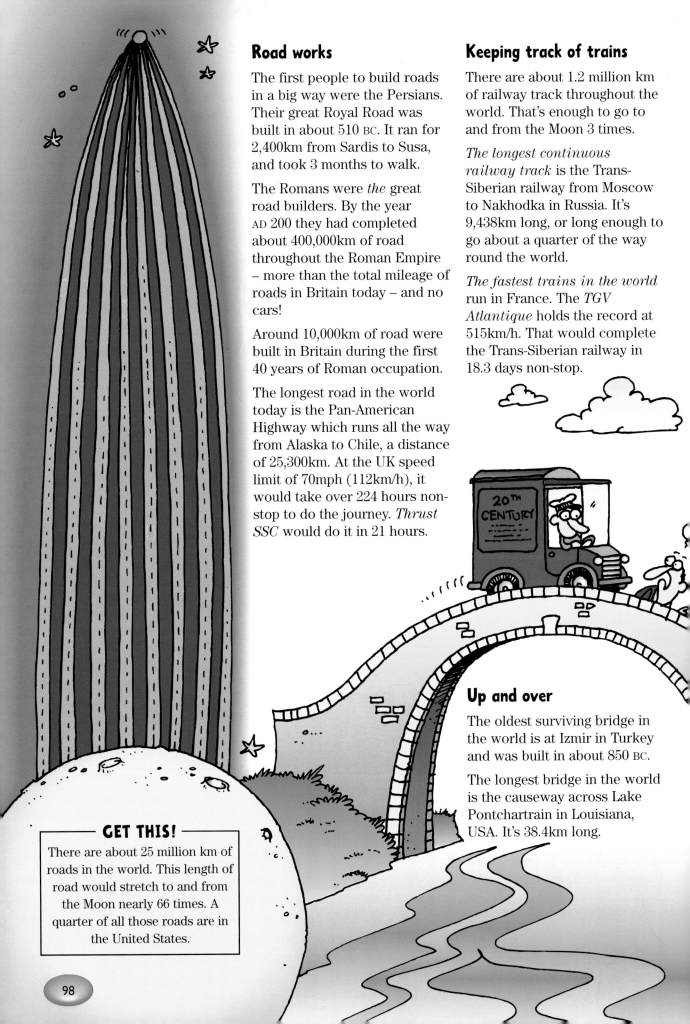

Dig this!

The first underground railway in the world was the Metropolitan Railway in London opened in 1863.

The London Underground system is the longest in the world with 401km of track. However, only about half of it is actually underground.

The longest transport tunnel in the world is the Seikan railway tunnel in Japan, built in 1988, which is 53.9km long.

The longest tunnel anywhere in the world is the water supply tunnel from New York City to Delaware, USA, which is 169km long – I wouldn't fancy swimming along it. When full, this tunnel contains 2.25 billion litres of water. That's 154 litres for every person living in New York, which means they could drink it dry in less than 3 months.

Up, up and away

We've long been taught that the first time man left the ground and travelled through the air was in 1783 when the Montgolfier brothers flew the first hot-air balloon. We are also taught that the first aeroplane was flown by the Wright brothers in 1903. But . . .

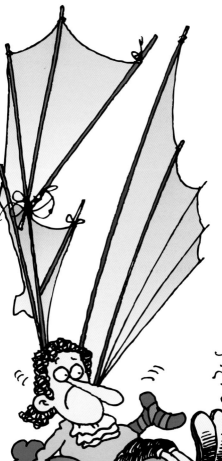

GET THIS!

In 1785 Jean-Pierre Blanchard became the first man to fly a balloon across the English Channel from England to France. To stop the balloon losing height, he and his companion had to throw everything overboard – including their trousers.

- Around AD 20, an inventor told the Chinese Emperor Wang Mang that he could fly over enemy cities and spy on them. The inventor flew several hundred metres with what was probably the world's first hang-glider.

- Clément Ader flew the first aeroplane near Paris on 9 October 1890, 13 years before the Wright brothers ever left the ground. He covered 50m. The first flight by the Wright brothers covered only 36.6m.

There were some less successful attempts at flight:

- In 1020 a Benedictine monk, Oliver of Malmesbury, attempted to fly from Malmesbury Abbey with the aid of wings, but ended up breaking his legs.

- In 1513 John Damian, physician to James IV of Scotland, plunged to his death when trying to fly from the walls of Stirling Castle.

- In 1742 the French nobleman the Marquis de Baqueville attempted to leap from his house in Paris and fly across the River Seine. He plummeted to the ground but fortunately landed in a washerwoman's boat and was saved by the dirty washing.

Whirly-gig

The helicopter was very difficult to build. Although Leonardo da Vinci first designed one in 1480, the first successful one to fly was not built until 1936. The earliest that one actually left the ground was in 1907. It had to be controlled on the ground by people with ropes and even then only reached the breathtaking height of 5cm.

Supersonic

The speed of sound in air is 1,195km/h, which means it takes about 8 seconds to travel a kilometre. That speed is called Mach 1. The first person to travel faster than that was the American test pilot, Chuck Yeager, in an X-1 rocket plane on 14 October 1947.

Faster than a bullet?

The fastest flight across the Atlantic was 1 hour 55 minutes, achieved in 1974 in a Lockheed SR-71A jet. The same jet holds the world air speed record of 3,608km/h. That's about as fast as a speeding bullet. A .22-calibre rifle bullet can reach 3,623km/h.

Concorde is the fastest passenger plane. It travels at 2,494km/h, which is twice the speed of sound. At that speed it would take just under 16 hours to fly around the world.

GET THIS!

When Concorde flies it becomes so warm that its body expands by almost 28cm.

Jumbo jumbo

A jumbo jet is equal to the weight of 67 African elephants – it's just as well elephants can't fly.

Alan Shepard from *Apollo 14* was the oldest man on the Moon, at 47 years 79 days. He was also the first to play golf on the Moon. Maybe you'll be the first to skateboard on the Moon!

The space shuttle weighs 2,000 tonnes and has to be launched at 28,000km/h in order to make it into space. When it lands it's still travelling at 350km/h and needs a runway over 11km long in which to stop.

First in space

The first creature in space was a dog, Laika, carried in *Sputnik 2* in 1957. Two mice, four monkeys, three more dogs and a rabbit also made it into space before man. However, man was the only one to come back!

The first man in space, Yuri Gagarin, who orbited the Earth in 1961, only reached a height of 327km, so was still within the Earth's ionosphere. He was in orbit for just 108 minutes.

Man did not go beyond the outer layer of atmosphere until Charles Conrad and Richard Gordon orbited the Earth in *Gemini 11* in 1966.

Only 12 people have walked on the Moon – all men and all American. The first was Neil Armstrong on 20 July 1969. The last was Eugene Cernan on 13 December 1972. Cernan spent the longest time on the Moon (22 hours).

Seriously fast

The fastest speed ever attained by humans is 39,897km/h by the crew of *Apollo 10* on their return to Earth in 1969. At that speed you'd circumnavigate the Earth in 1 hour!

The furthest man has ever travelled from the Earth is 400,171km, the distance reached by *Apollo 13* on its ill-fated trip in 1970.

The furthest a man-made object has ever travelled in space is over 10,500 million km and increasing every second. This is the distance reached by *Voyager 1*, which was launched in 1977.

Three other space-probes – *Pioneer 10*, *Pioneer 11* and *Voyager 2* – are also leaving the solar system. For the first time in our history, mankind has left home.

THE HUMAN TOUCH – PEOPLE AND PLACES

Humans have made a huge impact upon the planet and not all for the good. We've built huge cities, created countries and empires, waged wars and severely polluted the planet. And we've done all that in just 10,000 years.

The world has become so populated that if we're not careful, we'll run out of space to live and food to eat.

This section looks at some of the incredible facts about the impact of people and civilization on Planet Earth. We're going to look at how many people there are, where they are and what they've done!

Have you ever wondered ....
- how many people have ever lived
- where the loneliest place on Earth is
- when the most disastrous battle was fought
- who lives nearest the North Pole
- when today meets tomorrow

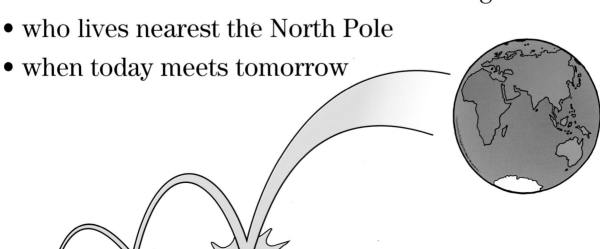

People, people, everywhere

About 6% of all the people who have ever lived are alive today.

There are now about 6 billion people on the Earth. To get some idea how much 6 billion people is, imagine if everyone in the world . . .

. . . linked hands and made a chain, side by side, arms outstretched – they would go round the Earth over 208 times.

. . . stood on each other's shoulders and formed a single column – it would stretch 9.27 million km or almost 25 times further than the Moon. (Unfortunately, lots of people would be crushed.)

. . . The total weight of every person living on the Earth is about 346 billion kg. That's the same as 66 Great Pyramids.

— GET THIS! —

The whole population of the world could be squeezed, with no room to move, on the island of Singapore (610 sq km). But only just. It would outgrow it within a year! And where would you go to the toilet!?

More and more

The world's population is increasing by 1.4% per year. It hasn't always increased at that rate.

In the year AD 1 the world's population was about 200 million.

It took 1,450 years to double to
    400 million

    310 years to double to 800 million

    140 years to double to 1,600 million

    63 years to double to 3,200 million

and it will take just 41 years to double to 6,400 million.

— GET THIS! —

Every hour there are 9,700 extra people on the Earth. That's the same as a new city the size of Manchester every fortnight!

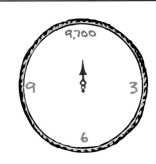

Gimme some elbow room

The most densely populated country in the world is Monaco, with 16,400 people per sq km. However, Monaco is really one small town and has a total size of only 1.95 sq km.

The most densely populated large country is Bangladesh with 986 people for every sq km. That's 4 times more densely populated than Britain.

The greatest concentration of humanity anywhere in the world, though, is in Hong Kong. There are parts of Kowloon where there are over 165,000 people per sq km. That's over 40 times worse than London, which has about 3,800 people for every sq km.

Growing and growing

Every third person in the world lives in either China (with 1,253 million people) or India (with 1,013 million people).

India's population is growing at almost twice the rate of China's. By the year 2028 India will be the most populated country in the world, – $\frac{1}{5}$ of the world's population will live there.

— GET THIS! —
Over half the world's population lives in just 6 countries: China, India, the United States, Indonesia, Brazil and Russia. Russia is the only one where the population figures are dropping.

Is there anybody there?

The country with the fewest people is Mongolia, which has only 1.7 people per sq km. That would be like the whole of Britain having the population of Bristol.

The region with the fewest people of all is Greenland, which has one person for every 37 sq km. Although over 85% of Greenland is always covered by ice, every person still has nearly 6 sq km of ice-free land. If the population of Britain was as thinly spread out only 82,000 people would live there and London would only have 380 people. You'd have no trouble getting on the tube then!

Lonely spots

The smallest community in the world is on Pitcairn Island in the Pacific. At last count only 44 people lived on its 5 sq km, most descended from the mutineers on the *Bounty*. It must be difficult getting a football team together.

The most remote community in the world is the town of Edinburgh on the island of Tristan da Cunha in the Atlantic Ocean. The population of 300 is 2,400km from their nearest neighbours – the 5,000 people living on the island of St Helena.

The world in their hands

The largest single country in the world is Russia with an area of 17,075,200 sq km, which is 11% of the total land surface of the Earth. It's 70 times larger than Britain.

GET THIS!

The largest territory ruled as a single country was the Mongol Empire established by Genghis Khan in 1206. Under Kublai Khan, from 1259 to 1294, it stretched from Hungary all the way to the Pacific Ocean, covering almost 16% of the Earth's land surface.

Teeny-tiny

The smallest country in the world is the Vatican City, which is a city within a city in Rome, Italy. It covers only 440,000 sq metres, just room for 40 football pitches.

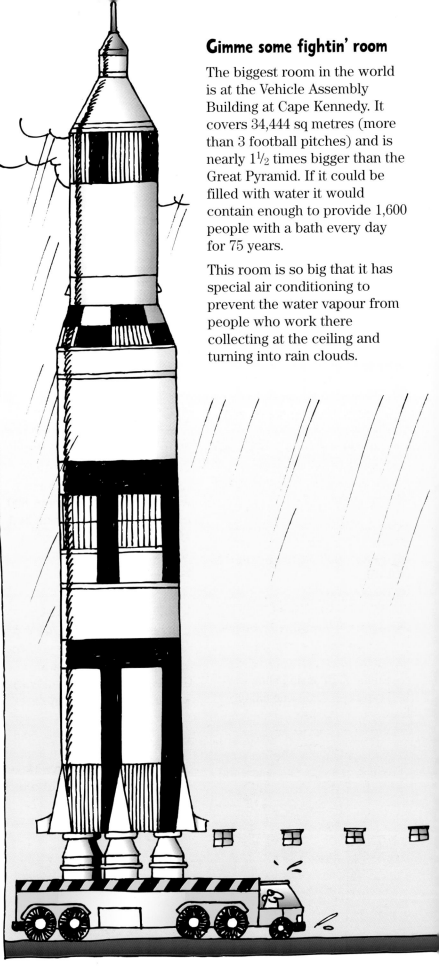

Gimme some fightin' room

The biggest room in the world is at the Vehicle Assembly Building at Cape Kennedy. It covers 34,444 sq metres (more than 3 football pitches) and is nearly 1½ times bigger than the Great Pyramid. If it could be filled with water it would contain enough to provide 1,600 people with a bath every day for 75 years.

This room is so big that it has special air conditioning to prevent the water vapour from people who work there collecting at the ceiling and turning into rain clouds.

Overload

When too many people live too close together disasters happen, disasters like plagues, famines and wars.

GET THIS!

The Black Death wiped out over $\frac{1}{3}$ of the population of Europe. An epidemic on that scale today would wipe out almost the entire United States of America.

Oldest and youngest countries

Only 2 modern countries have been in continuous existence for over 2,000 years – China, which was created from a number of warring states in 221 BC, and Japan, which traditionally dates its origin to 660 BC, although its first emperor actually ruled in 40 BC.

The shortest-lived country of recent years was Biafra, which survived for just 3 years, 1967–70, before being reconquered by Nigeria.

GET THIS!

In the whole history of mankind, no one had been born on Antarctica until 1978, when Emilio Marcos de Palma was born at an Argentine military base.

Disaster	When	Estimated number of deaths	% of world's population
Black Death	1347–51	75,000,000	18.5%
Famine in India	1770–1	10,000,000	1.1%
Cholera pandemic	1817–60	8,000,000	0.7%
Famine in China	1876–9	9,500,000	0.7%
World War I	1914–18	9,700,000	0.54%
Flu pandemic	1918	21,640,000	1.2%
Flooding of Hwang-He River	1931	3,700,000	0.2%
Russian famine	1930–4	13,000,000	0.62%
World War II	1939–45	54,800,000	2.38%

Hold your tongue!

The most commonly spoken language in the world is English, which is used by about 800 million people. However, it is the first language of only about 400 million people.

The most common 'native tongue' is Mandarin Chinese, which is spoken by about 800 million people, but if you add all the other Chinese dialects and languages, Chinese is spoken by over 1,250 million people.

There are about 6,000 different languages spoken in the world. About $\frac{1}{10}$ of them are spoken on just one island – New Guinea, in the western Pacific. School must be a nightmare.

Neighbours

China shares a border with 14 other countries. The border stretches for 22,113km. The total distance all the way round China is 37,346km.

If the population of China stood side by side and linked hands (and we allow them 1m of space) the 'Chinese chain' would go around their country about 34 times!

JOLLY GOOD!

Safety first

If you want to avoid crime, the safest place to live is Togo, in Africa, where less than 60 crimes were reported in 1997, or 11 for every 100,000 in the population.

The highest crime rate is in Surinam where there were over 17,800 crimes per 100,000 of the population – 1,620 times worse than Togo.

What's a lifetime?

In Britain the average lifetime is 75 years but in little Liechtenstein it's 81 and in Japan it's 79.

The shortest life expectancies are nearly all in Africa, with the poorest being Ethiopia, at only 38.

The world average is 63.

Be quiet!

The quietest natural place on Earth is deep underground in a cave.

The longest cave system is the Mammoth Cave in Kentucky, USA, which extends for over 530km. However, it gets so full of tourists that it is only quiet when closed for the night.

It is difficult to find anywhere totally quiet on the Earth's surface because sound is always created by the wind, by the wildlife or by mankind – usually planes flying overhead. The quietest place in the world, when it isn't windy, is the Antarctic, but there's nearly always a wind blowing.

The quietest place that isn't windy is the Kalahari Desert, but it isn't a nice place to be – Kalahari means 'suffering'.

Alternatively you could be becalmed in the Pacific Ocean.

A safer quiet place is a specially built sound-proof room at the Bell Telephone Laboratory in New Jersey, USA, which is capable of absorbing just about every sound.

Far and north

The furthest north you can go is the North Pole. Everywhere from there is south. But no one lives there. There is no land at the North Pole – just ice – and if all that ice melted, the North Pole would be in the middle of the sea.

The nearest land to the North Pole is Greenland, but the nearest settlement – the most northerly in the whole world – is at the radio and weather station at Alert, on the north of Ellesmere Island, Canada.

The most northerly town is Grise Fiord, also on Ellesmere Island. Only 150 people live there – but it still has a school – rats! It's 1,500km from the North Pole. Temperatures reach a high of 10°C in the summer but fall as low as –40°C in the winter – I hope the school has good central heating.

Far and south

The furthest south you can go is the South Pole, which is on land. There is a permanently staffed base there, but it is not a town as you and I think of it. There is no town on the whole of the Antarctic continent – though the research base at McMurdo Station, which is 1,184km from the South Pole, has about 1,200 scientists there in the summer and 200 in the winter. Do you have to be a mad scientist to stay there all winter?

The nearest proper settlement is Puerto Williams on Navarino Island at the most southerly point of Chile in South America. Only about 300 people live there. It's about 3,860km from the South Pole.

International date line

Far east and west

The furthest east you can go is the same as the furthest west. East and west are measured by imaginary lines of longitude which run from the North Pole to the South Pole. In 1884 it was agreed that all measurements of longitude would start from Greenwich, east of London, so this became 0° longitude. Everything was measured east and west from that point, which means they all come together around the other side of the Earth at 180° longitude. That line – known as the International Date Line – is where today becomes tomorrow!

GET THIS!

There are 2 islands very close to the Date Line – Big Diomede and Little Diomede in the Bering Strait between Alaska and Russia. They are only 3.2km apart. Anyone standing on Big Diomede, which is west of the Date Line, can look across into yesterday on Little Diomede.

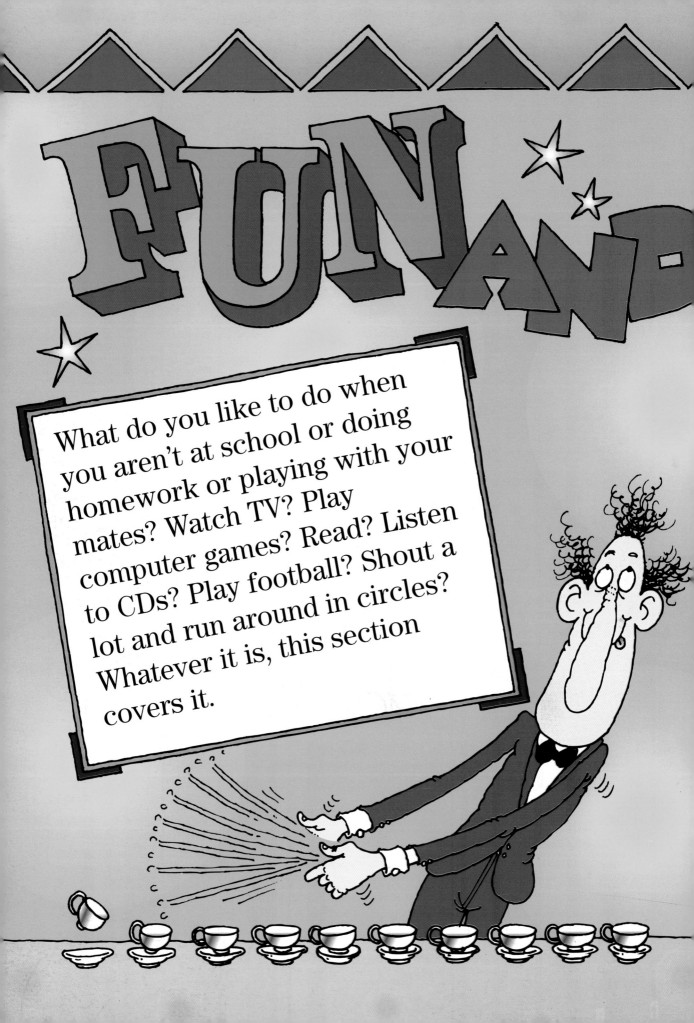

FUN AND

What do you like to do when you aren't at school or doing homework or playing with your mates? Watch TV? Play computer games? Read? Listen to CDs? Play football? Shout a lot and run around in circles? Whatever it is, this section covers it.

Head for heights

The longest bungee jump was by Gregory Riffi in 1992 from a helicopter. The bungee rope stretched to over 600m.

─ GET THIS! ─

The most spectacular stunt dive was 335m from near the top of the CN Tower in Toronto. It was done by Dar Robinson in 1979 for the film *Highpoint*. His safety parachute opened at 91m, or just 2 seconds before he would have hit the ground!

Watch out!

How far have you ever thrown, kicked or ejected anything? Could you rival these?

The furthest anyone has ever . . .
* fired an arrow – 1,854.4m – from a footbow
* struck a golf ball – 418.8m
* thrown a spear – 258.5m – from a Woomera
* thrown a frisbee – 200m
* thrown a baseball – 135.9m
* thrown a stone with a sling – 349.7m
* thrown a cricket ball – 128.6m
* thrown a javelin – 104.8m
* thrown a grape – 99.8m – it was caught by someone else in their mouth
* thrown an egg without breaking it – 98.5m – someone catches it!
* kicked a football – 97m
* thrown a cow-pat – 81m – the cow-pat was not fresh
* thrown their wellies – 64m – it was a size 8 boot!
* ejected (spitting) – 29m – a cherry stone

Snookered

While playing pool, Stuart Russell coughed and his false teeth flew out and went into the corner pocket. When he tried to get them out his arm got stuck and it took 2 police officers, 6 firemen and 50 customers to get him free!

Soccer stars

The fastest a goal has ever been scored in first-class football is 6 seconds. It's happened on 3 occasions, but the first was for Aldershot in 1958.

The highest score ever achieved in a first-class match was 36-0 when Arbroath beat Bon Accord in 1885!

Ricardinho Neves kept a ball off the ground by using his feet, legs or head for 19 hours 5½ minutes in 1994.

Keep on running

In 490 BC when the Persians invaded Greece, a Greek, Pheidippides, ran all the way from Athens to Sparta to seek help. The journey was 200km and it took him less than 2 days. He then ran back, took part in the battle, and ran from the battlefield to Athens – another 35km – to bring news of the victory. He ran 470km in 4 days and did a bit of fighting in between. No wonder he dropped dead. The name of the battle? The Battle of Marathon.

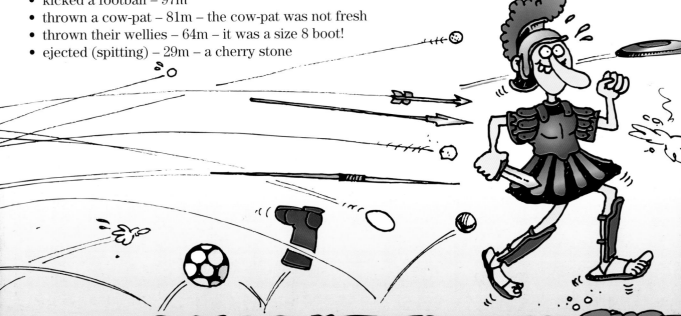

Beat this

The longest any single game has been played non-stop was a game of Monopoly that lasted for 264 hours over Christmas and New Year 1974–5.

In 1974 Gary Martin kept a yo-yo spinning for 55 hours.

The longest any football match has been played, with no substitutes, is 37 hours. It was between 2 American amateur teams in 1975.

The longest 2 people have fought each other is 11 hours 40 minutes, in a wrestling match between a Russian and a Finn in 1912.

On yer feet

The most stubborn endurance event must be the dancing marathon. In 1933, 2 dancers survived through a dancing marathon for 3,780 hours, or over 5 months.

Push off

In 1965 Chuck Linster did 6,006 press-ups in just under 4 hours without stopping. The most press-ups in 24 hours is 46,001. The most one-arm press-ups is 8,794 in 5 hours.

Hole in one

The longest distance from which anyone has ever scored a hole in one in golf is 409m.

Pile it on

The most people to ride a bicycle, all at the same time, is 17.

Tall boy

The highest stilts with which anyone has ever walked were 12.36m high. That's taller than the average house.

Basket case

In 1996 Ted St Martin scored 5,221 consecutive free throws in basketball.

Basketball player Wiley Peck slam-dunked a ball with such force that when it rocketed back up from the ground it hit Wiley on the chin and knocked him unconscious.

It's not fair

The 1932 Olympic Games were a bit unfair for some athletes.

- Jules Noël cast a very long discus throw but none of the officials was watching. Noël had to throw again, but produced a much poorer throw and ended up fourth.
- Hilda Strike came second in the women's 100m, beaten by Stella Walsh. However, it was discovered years later that Stella Walsh was actually a man.
- The steeplechase runners had to run an extra lap because the lap official forgot to change the lap counter.

GET THIS!

The only dead man ever to win a race was jockey Frank Hayes, who died while riding Sweet Kiss at Belmont Park in 1923. He remained in the saddle and was declared the winner before anyone realized he had died.

Early champs

The youngest ever world champion was Fu Mingxia of China who won the women's platform diving title in 1991 when she was 12.

The youngest world-record holder was Gertrude Ederle, who broke the 880-yard freestyle swimming record in 1919 when she was 12.

Dead slow

The top speed for a snail is 50.3m per hour. In the time it would take the snail to do a 100m dash, a sprint athlete could run over 700 100m races.

GET THIS!

Possibly the laziest of all sporting athletes was Blue Clip, the homing pigeon. In 1974, it took him 7 years 2 months to fly home from France to Manchester. The distance was 595km.

Towers of strength

The greatest weight lifted in a modern competition is 262.5kg, which is equal to lifting 4 full-grown men over your head at once. But there have been other amazing feats of strength.

- In 540 BC, Milo of Crotona, an Olympic wrestling champion, carried a full-grown ox, weighing about 1 tonne, for a distance of 180m.

- In 1891 Louis Cyr lifted 18 men seated on a platform on his back. The total weight was 1,950kg.

- In 1957 Paul Anderson lifted with his back a table laden with heavy metal parts weighing 2,845kg, the greatest weight lifted by a human.

Unique performers

- Jean Royer would swallow over 4½ litres of water and then gradually spew it out in an artistic arc while he quoted the 51st Psalm.

- Thea Alba was a remarkable German schoolgirl who could write different words at the same time with her hands, feet and mouth.

Record records

The best-selling single record of all time is *Candle in the Wind 1997* by Elton John, released at the time of Princess Diana's funeral. It has sold over 35 million copies.

It took 50 years for a single record to beat the previous best seller – *White Christmas* by Bing Crosby, although it's still the best-selling song.

The best-selling album of all time is *Thriller* by Michael Jackson, which has sold over 45 million copies – I bet your mum has a copy!

Groovy babies

The youngest person to have a hit record is Ian Doody, who went under the name Microbe. He was just 3 years old when his record *Groovy Baby* hit the charts in 1969.

The youngest person to have a painting at the Royal Academy was Gino Lyons. His painting *Trees and Monkeys* was painted when he was 3 and exhibited the day before his 5th birthday.

The youngest actor or actress to receive an Oscar was Shirley Temple who was 6 when she received a Special Award in 1934.

The youngest person to have a book published professionally was Dorothy Straight who wrote *How the World Began* when she was 4 – it was published in 1964 when she was 6.

On and on and on

If you listened to all of the music composed by Joseph Haydn just once, non-stop, it would take 340 hours, or over a fortnight. It would take 202 hours, or just over 8 days non-stop, to listen to everything Mozart composed, and 5 days for Beethoven.

The longest piece of music ever performed is the intensely monotonous *Sadist Factory* by Philip Crevier which goes on and on and on for 100 hours.

What's the point?

The quietest piece of music is *4 minutes 33 seconds* by John Cage. The title refers to the period of silence during which the musicians sit and listen to the audience.

The Nothing Book was full of nothing but blank pages and the film *Sleep* by Andy Warhol runs for 8 hours and just shows someone sleeping.

Perhaps the most pointless hobby was that of Francis Johnson who spent years ravelling together the biggest ball of string in the world. It stood over 3½m high and weighed nearly 9,600kg.

The letter 'e' is the most commonly used letter in the English language. As a challenge, in 1938, Ernest Vincent Wright wrote a 50,000-word novel, *Gadsby*, without once using the letter 'e'. The only trouble was his name – it had three 'e's in it!

Seriously tiny

The smallest book ever published measured just 1mm by 1mm. It was an edition of the nursery rhyme *Old King Cole* published in 1985. You need a needle to turn the pages.

The shortest record ever released is *The Mistake* by Dickie Goodman which lasts for just 1 second!

Suck that hoover

The humorist Gerard Hoffnung composed music for several household objects including vacuum cleaners and kettles.

The Brazilian composer Gilberto Mendes went even further, with music requiring electric shavers, an electric fan, a television set and cups and spoons. How do you think they played the electric fan?

Fun titles

Here are some fun song titles

- *I scream, you scream, we all scream for ice cream*
- *When there's tears in the eyes of a potato*
- *I've got tears in my ears from lying on my back in bed while I cry over you*
- *If you wanna leave me, can I come too?*
- *Harold the Hairy Ape*
- *Jeremiah Peabody's polyunsaturated quick-dissolving fast-acting pleasant-tasting green and purple pills*

Who's chicken?

One of Glenn Miller's best-known melodies is *In the Mood*. In 1977 Ray Stevens recorded it as the *Henhouse Five Plus Two* with the entire tune made up of chickens squawking.

Loudest music

The noisiest rock concert was the Monsters of Rock concert in 1988. The speakers belted out 250,000 watts of power and the sound of Eddie Van Halen could be heard over 30km away.

Longest word

The longest word in the Oxford English Dictionary has 45 letters – pneumonoultramicroscopicsilicovolcanoconiosis. It's an illness caused by breathing in fine quartz dust.

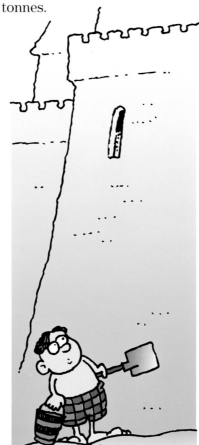

Marvellous models

Ever thought what you could do with your old Coke cans? In 1997, volunteers built a replica of St Peter's Basilica in Rome out of over 10 million empty aluminium cans. It was $\frac{1}{5}$ life size, and stood 29m high.

Syd Darnley of Sydney, Australia built an exact replica of Sydney Town Hall out of 74,000 seashells.

The world's biggest sandcastle is of Sleeping Beauty's Castle at Pacific Beach, San Diego. It's 12.25m high and weighs 15,000 tonnes.

Biggest pictures

The biggest painting ran on and on for over 3km. It was a panorama depicting nearly 2,000km of the Mississippi, painted by John Banvard in 1846. Unfortunately, it was destroyed in 1891.

The largest known portrait was cut into a wheat field by Stan Herd using a tractor! It covered 65 hectares and was a portrait of cowboy film star Will Rogers.

Fast work

If you could write as fast as these guys, maybe school would last half as long!

- Edward Judson, who created the name Buffalo Bill, claimed he wrote a 610-page book in 62 hours non-stop. That's 1 page every 6 minutes.

- Walter Gibson, who created the hero character 'The Shadow', produced a 40,000-word novel every week. He churned out 40 novels a year for almost 10 years.

Start again!

In 1835, after 5 months of hard struggle, Thomas Carlyle at last finished the first part of *The History of the French Revolution*. He lent it to a friend, and that friend lent it to another friend. That friend left it on a table and the next day the housemaid, thinking it was rubbish, lit the fire with it. Carlyle had no copy. He had to start all over again.

These days, of course, computers can lose entire books in a split second.

Movie madness

Here are some crazy gimmicks used to make going to the cinema more fun.

- *Smell-o-vision* – scents were piped into the cinema during the films

- *Horror horn* – a loud horn was sounded to warn the audience of a scary part

- *Quakorama* – seats were fitted with wheels that rocked at the appropriate moments

117

Bad to worse!

Here are some of the worst performers of all time.

Worst actor

Fellow actors of Robert Coates in the 1870s demanded police protection to appear on stage with him. At one 'serious' performance Coates, who was always covered in jewels and buttons, refused to leave the stage because he was hunting for a shoe buckle. The audience laughed so much that some needed treatment by a doctor.

Weirdest male singer

Herbert Khaury, better known as Tiny Tim, was a tall, ageing hippy with a high falsetto voice and was once known as the *singing canary*. He had a number of hit records but is best known for his squeaky rendition of *Tip-toe through the Tulips* in 1968.

Worst film

Plan 9 from Outer Space was directed by Ed Wood in 1959. Two aliens try to destroy Earth by raising the dead. Unfortunately the film's star, Bela Lugosi, died before the film was finished. Wood used a double who looked nothing like him – he stayed hidden behind a cloak for most of the film. Wood shot night scenes in full daylight and used car hubcaps and paper plates for flying saucers, clearly suspended by strings.

Worst female singer

Elva Miller could never sing in key or in time. Her voice has been described as the sound of 'cockroaches wrestling in a garbage can'. Yet when she recorded her version of Petula Clark's *Downtown* in 1965, it became a massive hit.

Worst orchestra

The Portsmouth Sinfonia, all amateurs, seldom ever hit the right notes or play together. It's often a gamble who'll finish first. Their version of the *1812 Overture* is even more of a disaster than the defeat of Napoleon that it's celebrating – yet people love their performances!

Who's who?

Some artists change their real name when they become actors or writers. Here's a few where you may understand why.

- Ellen Burstyn was Edna Gilhooley
- Michael Caine was Maurice Micklewhite
- Michael Crawford was Michael Dumble-Smith
- Boris Karloff was William Henry Pratt
- Robert Taylor was Spangler Brugh
- Conway Twitty was Harold Jenkins *(why change it?)*
- John Wayne was Marion Morrison

Essential reading

- *Engineering for Potatoes* by B.F. Cargill
- *Learning from Salmon* by Herman Aihara
- *Who's Who in Baton Twirling* by Don Sartellin
- *Enjoy Your Chameleon* by Earl Schneider
- *I Knew 3,000 Lunatics* by Victor R. Small
- *Aliens Ate my Trousers* by Hunt Emerson
- *Captain Underpants and the Attack of the Talking Toilets* by Dav Pilkey

Collecto-philes

The biggest collection of marbles numbers over 40,000.

People collect some weird stuff:
- aeroplane sickbags
- beer mats
- bubblegum packs
- cheese labels
- garden gnomes
- light bulbs
- sticking plasters (unused!)

Why, we wonder?

Special interests

There are some bizarre websites on the Internet:
- The Traffic Cone Preservation Society
- The Mango Appreciation Society
- The Nematode Songbook
- The Glacier Appreciation Society
- The Worm Page

Priceless!

The most valuable painting of all is believed to be the *Mona Lisa* by Leonardo da Vinci. It was estimated at £35 million in 1962. Experts are still arguing over who the Mona Lisa was – and what she was smiling about!

─ GET THIS! ─

The biggest library in the world is the Library of Congress in Washington DC, in the USA. It has about 28 million books and over 800km of shelves.

Million dollar book

The most anyone has ever paid for a book was $30.8 million (£19.2 million). It was for one of Leonardo da Vinci's notebooks known as *The Codex Hammer* and was bought by Bill Gates, founder of Microsoft, in 1994. What do you think your school books might be worth in 500 years' time?

Comic cash

Collecting comics is a serious business. Some issues are very rare and can fetch quite a price.

Action Comics No.1, June 1938 (first appearance of Superman)	£115,600
Detective Comics No. 27, May 1939 (first appearance of Batman)	£103,000
Marvel Comics No. 1, November 1939	£71,000
Superman No. 1, Summer 1939	£81,200
Batman No. 1, Spring 1940	£39,300
Beano No. 1, 1938	£6,000

ODDITIES AND ENTITIES

Some things are just plain odd, and you'd never believe they were true. Like people who enjoy getting up at 4.00 in the morning, or who enjoy homework!!!

In fact some things are even more odd than that. For the most incredible of the incredible here are some things that defy belief.

Helpful turtle

A young Korean boy fell overboard into the Pacific but was able to climb onto the back of a giant turtle. He was rescued 2 days later.

Lost ticket

When one man went to the doctor about his poor hearing they discovered he had a 47-year-old bus ticket wedged in his ear.

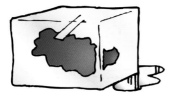

Poopsicles

It's not unusual for frozen poo to fall from the sky. When planes get rid of toilet refuse at very high altitudes it can sometimes freeze and fall as lumps of ice. This usually happens at sea but sometimes they hit land. A Kentucky farmer actually tasted one of these before he realized what it was!

What a way to go!

The Greek playwright Aeschylus apparently died when an eagle dropped a tortoise on his head.

In 1975 Alex Mitchell laughed so much while watching *The Goodies* comedy programme on television that he had a heart attack and died.

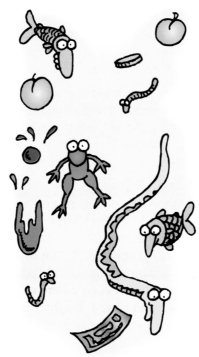

Raining cats and dogs

Over the years, hundreds of odd things have fallen from the sky. These include:

- live fish
- frogs
- toads
- mussels
- blood
- peaches
- hay
- snakes
- worms
- money

Master criminals

In 1974 Mrs Sharpe was mugged while she was taking her dog for a walk. The mugger snatched the bag Mrs Sharpe was carrying and drove away. It was only later he discovered that the bag contained dog poo!

In 1985 Christopher Logan, who was on trial for impersonating a policeman, escaped from the court by impersonating a policeman!

In 1989 Stephen Le tried to steal a pick-up truck but was stopped and chased. Le leaped over a fence to escape and then realized he'd escaped into San Quentin prison!

Half-baked beans

When police stopped a car in Colchester, Essex, in 1998, they were amazed to find the driver wearing wellington boots full of baked beans.

Barry Kirk, alias Captain Beany, lives his life as a baked bean. He wears an orange jumpsuit and cape and paints his bald head orange.

Truth or myth?

Some stories may or may not be true. They become what are called 'urban myths'.

In New York parents could no longer endure baby alligators as pets so flushed them down the toilet. Now, fully grown alligators live in the sewers under New York.

A man was trying to rescue his cat from a tree and tied a rope to a branch to pull the branch down to ground level. The rope broke, catapulting poor pussy into another garden where a mother and young daughter were praying for a new baby cat!

Shock treatment

In the Middle Ages it was believed that ringing church bells would stop thunderstorms. Unfortunately lightning often struck church steeples killing the bell-ringers who were holding on to wet ropes.

— GET THIS! —

In 1984 Larry Walters thought it would be fun to fly from his garden into his girlfriend's. He tied over 40 helium-filled balloons to a garden chair and shot 4,500m into the air. He was passed by several planes and became a hazard to air traffic. After 2 hours Walters drifted back to Earth but got entangled in overhead power lines, blacking out Long Beach, California! He was arrested and charged with 'flying in a reckless manner'.

— GET THIS! —

Legend has it that Jerome Cardano, the noted Italian astrologer, predicted the date of his own death – 2 September 1576. As he neared the appointed time he was still healthy, so he starved himself to death to fulfil his own prophecy.

Hold your breath

The longest attack of hiccups lasted for nearly 68 years until the victim, Charles Osborne, died in 1990, aged 95. He could never keep his false teeth in.

The longest attack of sneezing lasted for over 2 years 9 months. The victim, Donna Griffiths, sneezed over 2 million times.

Close shaves

In 1901 John Brown was within 1 minute of being hanged for murder when they discovered the wrong name was on the death warrant. Brown's sentence was changed to life imprisonment, but 12 years later the real murderer confessed to the crime and Brown was pardoned.

In 1941 William Wellman was just 2 minutes from death in the electric chair when another man confessed to the crime. Wellman's innocence was later proved and he was released.

The men they couldn't hang

In 1885, convicted murderer John Lee became famous as 'The Man they Couldn't Hang' when the trapdoor failed to open 3 times at his execution, even though it opened perfectly well when he wasn't standing on it. Instead he was imprisoned for life.

He wasn't the first. In 1803 they tried to hang murderer Joseph Samuels but the rope broke on each of the first 2 attempts and on the third the trapdoor failed to open. Samuels was set free.

Now where did I leave my?

Many items of lost property are found on buses and trains all over the world. Some of the oddest held by London Transport's Lost Property Office include:

- a box of false eyeballs
- an artificial leg
- a double bed
- a skeleton
- an outboard motor

Last post

The longest it's ever taken for a letter to be delivered is 110 years. It was posted in Tennessee in 1863 and was delivered in 1973 to a home for senior citizens in Detroit, where the person it was addressed to had once lived.

Brilliant babes

Some children display remarkable skills at an early age and are called child prodigies. What's your speciality?

- The composer Wolfgang Amadeus Mozart taught himself to play the harpsichord when he was 3, learned the violin when he was 7, and composed his first symphony when he was 8.

- Anthony McQuone of Weybridge, Surrey, could speak Latin and quote Shakespeare when he was only 2.

- Andragone DeMello spoke his first word when he was 7 weeks old; was playing chess at $2\frac{1}{2}$ and graduated from university with a maths degree when he was 10.

- Kim Ung-Yong of South Korea had the highest ever recorded IQ of 210 (150 is 'genius' level). He could speak 4 languages and perform integral calculus before he was 5.

GET THIS!

The greatest known horde of *buried treasure* is believed to be somewhere in the Cherokee Cave of Gold in Whitfield County, Georgia. It was discovered in 1890 by William Waterhouse, who was able to carry out only a few gold bars. But he couldn't find the cave again. The value of the horde is estimated to be about $10 billion.

Now who's clever?

Some people who may be mentally or physically impaired have other amazing abilities.

Stephen Wiltshire has only to glance at a building and he can draw it in minute detail.

Amazing twins

Twin brothers George and Charles can work out the day of the week for any date up to 40,000 years in the past or 40,000 years into the future. They can also remember the weather on every day of their lives. Once when a box of matches spilt open they both instantly said there were 111 before the matches hit the floor!

Speaking clock

A blind girl called Ellen always knew exactly what the time was, to the second, without having access to a clock. She had once listened to the speaking clock over the telephone and had continued to count the time ever after, precisely.

GET THIS!

At least 2 Japanese soldiers did not believe World War 2 had finished. Hiroo Onoda remained hidden in the forests of the Philippines until March 1974 and Teruo Nakamura continued to fight on the island of Morotai, Indonesia, until December 1974. Both believed news of the end of the war was a trick!

Odd bods

If you think some people you know are a bit odd, try some of these.

- Count Eric Stenbock had his meals while sitting in a coffin with a pet toad on his shoulder and a snake coiled around him.

- Prime Minister W.E. Gladstone went to bed with a hot-water bottle filled with tea. When he woke in the morning the tea was usually still warm, so he drank it.

- Field-Marshal Blücher was convinced he was going to give birth to an elephant. He was also sure that the floor of his house was heated to scalding temperatures so walked everywhere indoors on tiptoe.

- William Beckford, who was one of the richest men in Britain in the 1790s, loved to travel. On one occasion he took a flock of sheep with him to Portugal to improve the view from his window.

Weirdest house

Sara Winchester, of San José, California, was convinced that if she stopped making her house bigger, she would die, so she kept adding rooms. When she died in 1922, she had spent $5 million on one of the weirdest houses in the world. It has 160 rooms, some only inches wide, and a maze of staircases, some leading nowhere. There are 2,000 doors, 10,000 windows, 48 fireplaces and 9 kitchens.

Dead loss

The most hopeless suicide may well be Abel Ruiz of Madrid. He threw himself under a train but landed between the lines so the train passed over him. He jumped in front of a lorry but that stopped in time. After treatment Ruiz was talked out of his suicide attempts but upon leaving the hospital he was accidentally knocked down by a horse.

Absolutely hopeless

The world's worst army general may well have been Antonio Lopez de Santa Anna, the occasional President of Mexico.

- He was the victor at the Battle of the Alamo, but he lost over 1,500 men.
- After the Alamo he set up camp and ordered his men to take a siesta. They were promptly attacked by the enemy. Santa Anna fled the scene in his pyjamas.
- One clever scheme was to dress his men in the uniform of the enemy, but it all went horribly wrong because no one knew which side anyone was on.
- Santa Anna lost a leg at the battle of Vera Cruz in 1838 but kept the leg with him for 4 years until he was able to give it a state funeral.
- He lost his artificial leg in another battle. Santa Anna had crept away to have a crafty chicken lunch. He was surprised by some American soldiers and fled the scene leaving his leg behind. It's now on display at the Illinois State Military Museum.

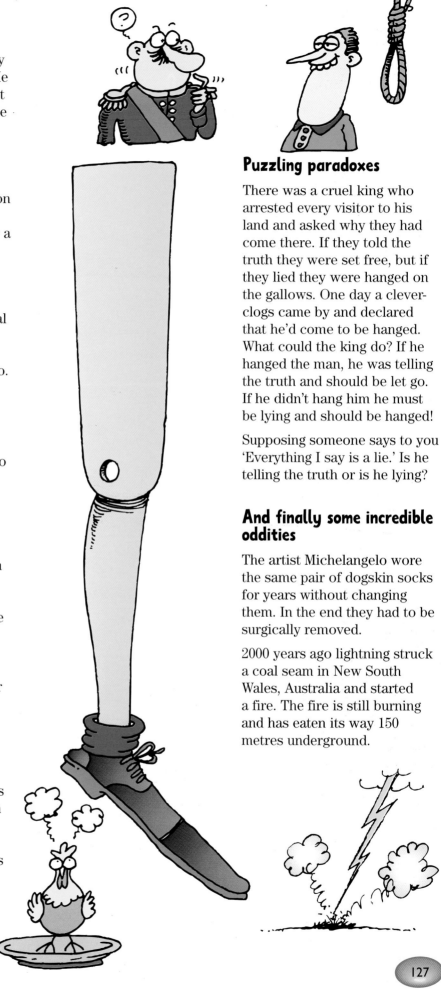

Puzzling paradoxes

There was a cruel king who arrested every visitor to his land and asked why they had come there. If they told the truth they were set free, but if they lied they were hanged on the gallows. One day a clever-clogs came by and declared that he'd come to be hanged. What could the king do? If he hanged the man, he was telling the truth and should be let go. If he didn't hang him he must be lying and should be hanged!

Supposing someone says to you 'Everything I say is a lie.' Is he telling the truth or is he lying?

And finally some incredible oddities

The artist Michelangelo wore the same pair of dogskin socks for years without changing them. In the end they had to be surgically removed.

2000 years ago lightning struck a coal seam in New South Wales, Australia and started a fire. The fire is still burning and has eaten its way 150 metres underground.

Index

a acids, 70
aeroplanes, 67,100
aliens, 75
ancient history, 82–7
animals, 20–41
Antarctic, 31,58,63,92,95,107–8
Arctic, 31,93,108
asteroids, 49
astronauts, 70,101
athletes, 112–14
atmosphere, 62
atoms, 10,67
avalanches, 63

b bacteria, 24,26–7,31,35,70
baked beans, 123
balloons, 99
bamboo, 22
battles and wars, 86–7,125
bees, 29,78
beetles and bugs, 24–5,26,29,31
bicycles, 97,113
Big Bang, 47
Biggest things, 22,24,36–8,44,54,69,96,106, 117,119
birds, 24,25–6,28,31,38,41,114
black holes, 47
blood, 16
boats, 92,96
bones, 12,14
books, 115–17,119
brains, 10
bridges, 98
bugs, *see beetles*
buildings, 84–5,106
butterflies and moths, 25,28–9

c camels, 25
canyons, 55
cars, 97
cats, 28,86
caves, 56,108,125
cells, 10–12,24
chickens, 31,38
children, 18,19,76,86,114–5,124–5
cities, 82
cliffs, 55
close shaves, 124
coastline, 55
coincidences, 76–7
coldest things, 50,62,68
comets, 46,50
comics, 119
computers, 70
Concorde, 44,100
continents, 57
countries, 55,82,105–7
creepy-crawlies, 25,27,29,31,35
criminals, 108,122

d deserts, 58,108
dinosaurs, 32–41,79
disappearances, 75,94
disasters, 107
diseases, 70,107
dogs, 31
dreams, 19

e ears, 14
Earth, 34,53–63
earthquakes, 59
eccentrics, 87,115,118,123,126–7
elements, 67–8
elephants, 14,24,26,101
explorers, 92–3,94–5
eyes, 14

f falling, 67,112,
fastest things, 26,38,44–5,66–7,96–8, 100–1,112
fears, 18
films, 117–18
fish, 22,25,27,30,35
flight, 26,28,99
food, 16,17
football, 112
frogs, 30
fungus, 30

g galaxies, 44
games, 112–13
geysers, 59
ghosts, 74
gold, 60
gravestones, 89
greasy bits, 12

h hair, 14–15
heart, 16
heaviest things, 19,22,36,54
heroes, 83
hibernate, 31
highest points, 56,57
holes, 56
hottest things, 31,47–8,50,56,62,69
human body, 8–19,68
humans, early, 82,92

i insects, 25–7,29,31,35
inventions, 71,82
islands, 54–5,109

j jellyfish, 30
jumping, 26,112

k kangaroo, 25
kings & queens, 86–8

l lakes, 60
languages, 88,107
last words, 88
light speed, 44,66
lightest things, 19
lightning, 63
lobsters, 28
longest things, 55,57,60,97–9,112–13, 117,124
lost property, 124
lungs, 16

m memory, 19
migration, 28
miracles, 77
mistakes, 70
models, 117
monsters, 32,35–41,75
Moon, 48
mountains, 56–7
mucus, 13,16
muscles, 11,14
music, 115–16
mysteries, 73–9

n nails, 15
nastiest people, 83,87
nerves, 11
noisiest things, 22,55,58
nose, 13
numbers, 69

o oceans, 56,60,108
oddest things, 122–7
oldest things, 19,23,27,34,82,87,107
outer space, *see space*

p paradoxes, 127
penguins, 26,31
people, 19,104–5
phobias, 18

pictures, 117
planets, 44–5,48–50
plants, 20–5,30
poo, 16,122
population, 81,104–5
predictions, 78–9,123
pyramids, 23,84

q quietest things, 108

r railways, 98–9
rain, 62
remotest places, 55,105,108
richest people, 106,119
rivers, 60
roads, 98

s saliva, 13
scientists, 70,71,82
seas, 60,92
seaside, 55
seaweed, 22
sharks, 26,68
sheep, 31,68
shortest things, 19,107
skin, 12
slowest things, 26,114
smallest things, 14,19,24,87,105–6
smelliest things, 13,30,68,87
snakes, 25,30
snow, 63
sound, 14,66
space, 42–51
space travel, 44,70,101
speed, 26,44,46,66,100–1
spiders, 29
spit, 13
sports, 96–7,112–14
squid, 22
stars, 44,47
stomach, 17
storms, 63
strongest things, 11,114
Sun, 44,47
sweat, 12

t tallest things, 19,23,56,85
thunder, 63
time, 47,79,109
tongue, 13
tornadoes, 63
traffic, 97
trains, 13, 98–9
transport, 91,96–101
treasure, 124
trees, 23
tunnels, 99
twins, 77,125

u Universe, 44,47
unknown creatures, 75,79

v volcanoes, 39,49,50,58,71
vomit, 18

w walking, 91–2,94–5
wars, *see battles*
water, 12,60,68
waterfalls, 61
waves, 55
weather, 62–3
wettest things, 61,62
whales, 22,25,28
winds, 50,63
words, 88,115,116
worms, 22,35

An 8 tonne elephant is equal to 8,000,000 Smarties.
The tallest tree is 770 Smarties tubes high.